# HARCOURT

# Math

# Practice Workbook

## PUPIL'S EDITION
### Grade 3

**Harcourt**

Orlando • Boston • Dallas • Chicago • San Diego
www.harcourtschool.com

## California Edition

Printed in the United States of America

ISBN 0-15-320437-0

17 18 19    073    2009    2008    2007

© Harcourt

# CONTENTS

Name _____

# Compare Numbers

Compare the numbers. Write $<$, $>$, or $=$ in the $\bigcirc$.

1. 256 $\bigcirc$ 266

2. 138 $\bigcirc$ 136

3. 161 $\bigcirc$ 116

4. 355 $\bigcirc$ 365

5. 856 $\bigcirc$ 856

6. 44 $\bigcirc$ 444

7. 3,456 $\bigcirc$ 3,456

8. 81 $\bigcirc$ 80

## Mixed Review

Write the number in standard form.

9. $40,000 + 6,000 + 300 + 50 + 5$ _____

10. $20,000 + 700 + 20 + 9$ _____

11. eight thousand, three hundred fifty-two _____

12. forty-three thousand, six hundred twenty-five _____

Write the number in expanded form.

13. 17,045 _____

14. 59,811 _____

15. 4,906 _____

Complete the pattern.

16. 25, 30, 35, ___, ___

17. 17, 20, 23, ___, ___

18. 52, 54, 56, ___, ___

19. 21, 28, ___, 42, ___

# Order Numbers

Write the numbers in order from *least* to *greatest*.

440    445    450    455    460    465    470

1. 445, 451, 450          2. 456, 449, 468          3. 470, 462, 468

_____          _____          _____

210 220 230 240 250 260 270 280 290 300 310

4. 221, 210, 235          5. 305, 275, 255          6. 246, 232, 310

_____          _____          _____

1,000 2,000 3,000 4,000 5,000 6,000 7,000 8,000 9,000

7. 2,326; 1,503; 3,235    8. 5,609; 5,950; 4,999    9. 9,000; 7,607; 4,439

_____          _____          _____

Write the numbers in order from *greatest* to *least*.

10. 165, 132, 169          11. 87, 110, 56          12. 254, 124, 304

_____          _____          _____

## Mixed Review

Solve.

13. $29 + 10 + 4 =$ _____          14. $71 + 12 + 8 =$ _____

15. $53 + 11 + 14 =$ _____          16. $72 + 8 + 0 =$ _____

17. $13 + 58 + 29 =$ _____          18. $49 + 49 + 10 =$ _____

19.  $\begin{array}{r} 79 \\ -31 \\ \hline \end{array}$      20.  $\begin{array}{r} 98 \\ -37 \\ \hline \end{array}$      21.  $\begin{array}{r} 49 \\ -19 \\ \hline \end{array}$      22.  $\begin{array}{r} 60 \\ -20 \\ \hline \end{array}$

© Harcourt

**PW8   Practice**

# Round to Nearest 1,000

Round to the nearest thousand.

1. 2,345 _____  2. 1,765 _____  3. 8,821 _____

4. $6,109 _____  5. 3,001 _____  6. $3,679 _____

7. 9,134 _____  8. $4,556 _____  9. 7,733 _____

Round to the nearest thousand, the nearest hundred, and the nearest ten.

10. 3,490 _____ _____ _____

11. 7,509 _____ _____ _____

12. $2,565 _____ _____ _____

13. 3,115 _____ _____ _____

14. 1,350 _____ _____ _____

15. 8,999 _____ _____ _____

16. $6,784 _____ _____ _____

17. 2,288 _____ _____ _____

18. $5,501 _____ _____ _____

## Mixed Review

Write the value of the underlined digit.

19. 4,5$\underline{2}$3 _____  20. $\underline{1}$3,886 _____  21. 60,$\underline{6}$00 _____

22. $\underline{3}$27 _____  23. 68$\underline{7}$ _____  24. $\underline{2}$2,789 _____

Solve.

|  | 25. | 26. | 27. | 28. |
|---|---|---|---|---|
|  | 68 | 86 | 49 | 92 |
|  | −45 | −70 | +13 | −31 |

# Column Addition

Find the sum.

1. $(2 + 5) + 3 =$ _____ 　　2. $6 + (3 + 5) =$ _____ 　　3. $(4 + 5) + 9 =$ _____

4. $4 + (13 + 7) =$ _____ 　　5. $(4 + 3) + 6 =$ _____ 　　6. $(1 + 7) + 14 =$ _____

7. $12 + (6 + 6) =$ _____ 　　8. $(14 + 6) + 3 =$ _____ 　　9. $7 + (10 + 5) =$ _____

Use the Grouping Property to find the sum.

| 10. | 11. | 12. | 13. |
|---|---|---|---|
| 2 | 4 | 22 | 14 |
| 4 | 1 | 13 | 10 |
| + 6 | + 9 | + 8 | + 16 |

| 14. | 15. | 16. | 17. |
|---|---|---|---|
| 25 | 33 | 21 | 23 |
| 14 | 44 | 34 | 18 |
| + 26 | + 17 | + 45 | + 12 |

## Mixed Review

Round to the nearest hundred.

18. 456 　　　　19. 301 　　　　20. 3,698 　　　　21. 4,022

_____ 　　　_____ 　　　_____ 　　　_____

22. 678 　　　　23. 1,103 　　　　24. 5,833 　　　　25. 6,666

_____ 　　　_____ 　　　_____ 　　　_____

Solve.

26. $12 + 33 =$ _____ 　　27. $44 - 20 =$ _____ 　　28. $17 + 15 =$ _____

29. $25 - 13 =$ _____ 　　30. $40 + 30 =$ _____ 　　31. $42 - 19 =$ _____

# Estimate Sums

Estimate the sum.

| 1. | 2. | 3. | 4. |
|---|---|---|---|
| 23 | 44 | 69 | 429 |
| +71 | +33 | +12 | +258 |

| 5. | 6. | 7. | 8. |
|---|---|---|---|
| $1.32 | 4,367 | $6.65 | 1,252 |
| +$2.48 | +5,717 | +$1.99 | +2,834 |

For 9–11 use the numbers at the right.

9. Choose two numbers whose sum is about 80.

_____

10. Choose two numbers whose sum is about 4,000.

_____

11. Choose two numbers whose sum is about 700.

_____

| 533 |
|---|
| 38 |
| 1,092 |
| 41 |
| 229 |
| 3,481 |

## Mixed Review

Write <, >, or = for each ◯.

12. 334 ◯ 443     13. 4,980 ◯ 4,098

14. 814 ◯ 814     15. 39 ◯ 31

Write each number in standard form.

16. 60,000 + 2,000 + 500 + 50 _____

17. forty-three thousand, nine hundred sixty-six _____

18. 2,000 + 900 + 40 + 3 _____

19. eighty thousand, two hundred eleven _____

20. 70,000 + 300 + 70 + 9 _____

Name _____

# Add 3-Digit Numbers

Use base-ten blocks to find each sum.

1.  341
   +237

2.  832
   +138

3.  426
   +427

4.  359
   +196

5.  532
   +389

6.  644
   +317

7.  277
   +235

8.  442
   +469

9.  353
   +588

10. 527
   +197

11. 438
   +279

12. 377
   +195

13. 159
   +262

14. 349
   +464

15. 618
   +329

16. 627
   +326

17. 378
   +577

18. 819
   +153

19. 377
   +188

20. 429
   +469

## Mixed Review

Add.

21. 57
   +36

22. 88
   +97

23. 49
   +57

24. 67
   +38

25. 49
   +89

Subtract.

26. 57
   −32

27. 98
   −84

28. 69
   −57

29. 58
   −38

30. 99
   −81

31. 92
   −18

32. 14
   − 8

33. 76
   −54

34. 29
   −14

35. 78
   −26

© Harcourt

# Add Greater Numbers

Find the sum. Estimate to check.

1.  2,341
    +6,237

2.  1,861
    +6,733

3.  7,849
    +3,259

4.  1,776
    +1,954

5.  1,952
    +1,980

6.  1,988
    +1,982

7.  1,113
    +5,988

8.  7,182
    +1,939

9.  4,594
    +3,534

10. 6,318
    +4,916

11. 7,657
    +1,284

12. 4,594
    +8,475

13. 4,588
    +5,455

14. 5,387
    +8,347

15. 3,425
    +5,456

16. 6,859
    +1,346

## Mixed Review

Write the numbers in order from *least* to *greatest*.

17. 245, 253, 232

18. 350, 345, 319

19. 632, 599, 900

_____    _____    _____

Add.

20. (3 + 4) + 4 = ____

21. (4 + 5) + 7 = ____

22. (1 + 6) + 9 = ____

23. (6 + 4) + 7 = ____

24. (8 + 8) + 3 = ____

25. (7 + 4) + 8 = ____

26. (9 + 2) + 5 = ____

27. (6 + 7) + 4 = ____

28. (8 + 1) + 7 = ____

29. 221
    +876

30. 595
    +111

31. 469
    +568

32. 670
    +710

# Estimate Differences

Estimate the difference.

1.  $\begin{array}{r} 836 \rightarrow \underline{\phantom{000}} \\ -328 \rightarrow -\underline{\phantom{000}} \end{array}$

2.  $\begin{array}{r} 59 \rightarrow \underline{\phantom{000}} \\ -19 \rightarrow -\underline{\phantom{000}} \end{array}$

3.  $\begin{array}{r} \$7.63 \rightarrow \underline{\phantom{000}} \\ -\$1.88 \rightarrow -\underline{\phantom{000}} \end{array}$

4.  $\begin{array}{r} 8{,}909 \rightarrow \underline{\phantom{000}} \\ -2{,}408 \rightarrow -\underline{\phantom{000}} \end{array}$

5.  $\begin{array}{r} 6{,}851 \rightarrow \underline{\phantom{000}} \\ -2{,}055 \rightarrow -\underline{\phantom{000}} \end{array}$

6.  $\begin{array}{r} 566 \rightarrow \underline{\phantom{000}} \\ -377 \rightarrow -\underline{\phantom{000}} \end{array}$

7.  $\begin{array}{r} \$12.78 \rightarrow \underline{\phantom{000}} \\ -\$\ 8.49 \rightarrow -\underline{\phantom{000}} \end{array}$

8.  $\begin{array}{r} 379 \rightarrow \underline{\phantom{000}} \\ -119 \rightarrow -\underline{\phantom{000}} \end{array}$

9.  $\begin{array}{r} \$8.17 \rightarrow \underline{\phantom{000}} \\ -\$5.51 \rightarrow -\underline{\phantom{000}} \end{array}$

10. $\begin{array}{r} 874 \rightarrow \underline{\phantom{000}} \\ -188 \rightarrow -\underline{\phantom{000}} \end{array}$

11. $\begin{array}{r} 5{,}501 \rightarrow \underline{\phantom{000}} \\ -3{,}288 \rightarrow -\underline{\phantom{000}} \end{array}$

12. $\begin{array}{r} \$6.93 \rightarrow \underline{\phantom{000}} \\ -\$2.64 \rightarrow -\underline{\phantom{000}} \end{array}$

## Mixed Review

Write the missing number.

13. 8, 13, _____, 23, 28    14. 16, 23, 30, 37, _____    15. _____, 20, 29, 38, 47

Write the value of the underlined digit.

16. 5̲3,980 _____    17. 46,8̲31 _____    18. $3̲67.15 _____

Add.

19. $\begin{array}{r} 3{,}400 \\ +\ \ \ 54 \\ \hline \end{array}$

20. $\begin{array}{r} 1{,}209 \\ +\ 530 \\ \hline \end{array}$

21. $\begin{array}{r} 1{,}050 \\ +\ 803 \\ \hline \end{array}$

22. $\begin{array}{r} 7{,}674 \\ +\ 3{,}421 \\ \hline \end{array}$

23. 54 + 24 = _____    24. 17 + 39 = _____    25. 31 + 31 = _____

© Harcourt

# Subtract Greater Numbers

Find the difference. Estimate to check.

| 1. | 2. | 3. | 4. | 5. |
|---|---|---|---|---|
| 1,500<br>−1,132 | 1,406<br>−1,258 | 1,600<br>−1,198 | 2,902<br>−2,435 | 2,700<br>−1,137 |

| 6. | 7. | 8. | 9. | 10. |
|---|---|---|---|---|
| 3,408<br>−2,135 | 4,800<br>−1,654 | 3,306<br>−3,108 | 6,300<br>−2,229 | 8,200<br>−5,777 |

11. $7,005 - 3,605 =$ _____  12. $8,588 - 5,666 =$ _____

13. $2,175 - 1,987 =$ _____  14. $6,921 - 4,108 =$ _____

## Mixed Review

Find each sum or difference.

15. $19 + 6 =$ _____  16. $78 - 49 =$ _____

17. $84 - 27 =$ _____  18. $29 + 54 =$ _____

Find the missing addend.

19. $60 -$ _____ $= 24$  20. $71 -$ _____ $= 35$

21. $17 +$ _____ $= 58$  22. $42 +$ _____ $= 79$

Find each sum.

23. $996 + 132 =$ _____  24. $4,597 + 1,950 =$ _____

25. $3,956 + 2,007 =$ _____  26. $774 + 2,981 =$ _____

27. Which number is between 4,888 and 6,123?

  A 5,030    C 1,325

  B 7,548    D 3,987

28. Which symbol completes the following:
    $4,620 \bigcirc 4,062$

  F >    G <    H =

# Problem Solving Skill

## Estimate or Exact Answer

Use the table for 1–2. Write whether you need an exact answer or an estimate. Then solve.

| Bulbs by the Bag | |
|---|---|
| Item | Price |
| tulips | $4.67 |
| daffodils | $2.39 |
| irises | $3.99 |

1. Justin has $8. Can he buy a bag of tulips and a bag of irises?

   _____

   _____

2. Roxana pays for a bag of daffodils with $3. How much change will she get?

   _____

Derek is planning to plant two types of flower bulbs. He has 39 tulip bulbs and 18 daffodil bulbs.

3. Derek wants to put a stick in the ground where he plants each bulb. Which sentence shows how many sticks he must have?
   - A  39 + 18 = 57
   - B  40 + 20 = 60
   - C  40 + 18 = 58
   - D  39 − 18 − 21

4. After Derek plants the bulbs, he wants to pour at least 1 cup of water on each bulb. Which container should he fill with water?
   - F  one that holds 30 cups
   - G  one that holds 40 cups
   - H  one that holds 60 cups
   - J  one that holds 80 cups

## Mixed Review

Solve.

5.  364
   −291

6.  109
   +637

7.  518
   −462

8.  279
   +584

# Write Expressions and Number Sentences

Write an expression for each.

1. Garnet bought 16 red buttons, 8 blue buttons, and 25 green buttons. How many blue and red buttons did she buy?

2. Kay has 13 more sheets of lined paper than unlined paper. She has 26 sheets of unlined paper. How many sheets of lined paper does she have?

_____

_____

3. Lyle has 152 minutes of recording time on a tape. He uses 65 minutes. How much time does he have left?

4. Neil had 35 cookies. He gave 26 cookies to his classmates. How many cookies does he have left?

_____

_____

Write $+$ or $-$ to make the number sentence true.

5. $4 \bigcirc 2 = 2$

6. $27 = 18 \bigcirc 9$

7. $32 \bigcirc 3 = 35$

8. $67 = 7 \bigcirc 60$

9. $39 \bigcirc 16 = 55$

10. $16 \bigcirc 11 = 5$

11. $15 \bigcirc 7 = 8$

12. $50 = 61 \bigcirc 11$

13. $71 = 43 \bigcirc 28$

Write the missing number that makes the number sentence true.

14. $9 + \underline{\hspace{1cm}} = 21$

15. $8 = \underline{\hspace{1cm}} - 9$

16. $\underline{\hspace{1cm}} + 81 = 93$

17. $160 = 50 + \underline{\hspace{1cm}}$

18. $\underline{\hspace{1cm}} - 123 = 16$

19. $36 - \underline{\hspace{1cm}} = 5$

20. $57 + 18 = \underline{\hspace{1cm}}$

21. $115 - 113 = \underline{\hspace{1cm}}$

22. $237 - \underline{\hspace{1cm}} = 195$

## Mixed Review

Find each sum.

23.  $\begin{array}{r} 2 \\ 7 \\ +9 \\ \hline \end{array}$

24.  $\begin{array}{r} 3 \\ 6 \\ +8 \\ \hline \end{array}$

25.  $\begin{array}{r} 5 \\ 4 \\ +7 \\ \hline \end{array}$

26.  $\begin{array}{r} 8 \\ 8 \\ +3 \\ \hline \end{array}$

# Make Equivalent Sets

## Vocabulary

Complete the sentence.

1. Sets that are _____ name the same amount.

Make an equivalent set for each amount. List the bills and coins
you used.

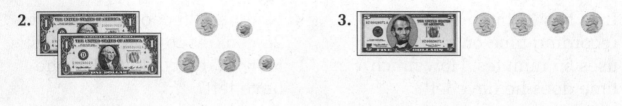

2. _____          3. _____

_____          _____

Make three equivalent sets for each amount. List the bills and coins you
used.

4. $1.60                                    5. $6.50

_____          _____

_____          _____

_____          _____

## Mixed Review

Round to the nearest hundred.

6. 84 _____          7. 359 _____          8. 866 _____

9. 91 _____          10. 499 _____          11. 601 _____

12. Which digit is in the thousands place of 2,617? _____

13. Which digit is in the hundreds place of 8,310? _____

14. Which digit is in the thousands place of 19,036? _____

# Problem-Solving Stategy

## Make a Table

Make a table to solve.

1. Ivy has two $1 bills, 4 quarters, 7 dimes, 1 nickel, and 4 pennies to buy a pack of paper that costs $2.66. How many different equivalent sets of bills and coins can she use?

_____

| | | | | | |
|---|---|---|---|---|---|
| | | | | | |
| | | | | | |
| | | | | | |
| | | | | | |

2. How many combinations of coins can you use to make 23¢?

_____

| | | | |
|---|---|---|---|
| | | | |
| | | | |
| | | | |
| | | | |
| | | | |
| | | | |
| | | | |
| | | | |
| | | | |
| | | | |

## Mixed Review

Add.

| 3. | 152 | 4. | 87 | 5. | 136 | 6. | 101 |
|---|---|---|---|---|---|---|---|
| | 63 | | 84 | | 242 | | 345 |
| | + 256 | | + 75 | | + 192 | | + 72 |

| 7. | 49¢ | 8 | $1.25 | 9. | 17¢ | 10. | 29¢ |
|---|---|---|---|---|---|---|---|
| | + 26¢ | | + $0.75 | | + 66¢ | | + 50¢ |

# Compare Amounts of Money

Use > or < to compare the amounts of money.

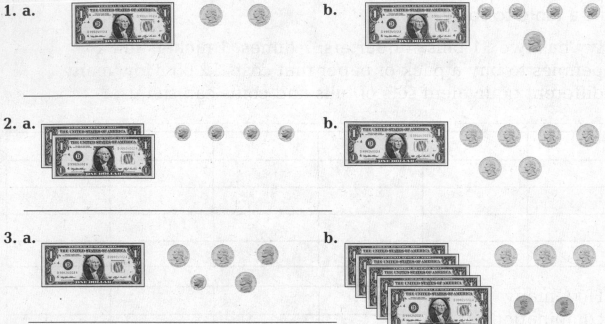

1. a. _____  b.

2. a. _____  b.

3. a. _____  b.

## Mixed Review

4. Continue the pattern.

   19, 29, 39, 49, _____, _____, _____

Find the sum.

| 5. | 85 | 6. | 14 | 7. | 565 | 8. | 26 |
|----|----|----|----|----|-----|----|----|
|    | 72 |    | 33 |    | + 128 |  | 38 |
|    | + 21 |  | + 67 |  |     |    | + 52 |

9. What is the value of the underlined digit in 10,7̲29?

   A 70                     C 7,000

   B 700                    D 70,000

10. What is the value of the underlined digit in 18,̲246?

   A 80                     C 8,000

   B 800                    D 80,000

Name _____

## Make Change

List the coins you would get as change from a $1 bill.
Use play money.

**1.** $0.92    **2.** $0.35   **3.** $0.59

_____   _____   _____

_____   _____   _____

Complete the table. Use play money.

| | Amount Paid | Cost of Item | Change |
|---|---|---|---|
| **4.** | $1.00 | $0.19 | |
| **5.** | $5.00 | $2.73 | |
| **6.** | $6.00 | $5.31 | |

## Mixed Review

Find the sum or difference.

**7.**   264
    + 599

**8.**   3,672
    − 1,488

**9.**   4,628
    − 1,999

**10.**   2,870
    + 9,653

**11.** Order these numbers from least to greatest.
    3,876      3,678      3,768

_____

**12.** What is one hundred more than 7,409?

_____

**13.** What is the standard form of five thousand two hundred
    seventeen?

_____

Name _____

# Add and Subtract Money

Find the sum or difference. Estimate to check.

1.  $6.43
   +$2.15

2.  $5.63
   −$1.50

3.  $2.59
   +$1.37

4.  $4.93
   −$1.78

5.  $0.38
   +$5.24

6.  $3.27
   +$2.06

7.  $6.55
   −$4.90

8.  $4.02
   −$3.91

9.  $3.50
   −$1.98

10.  $1.90
    +$2.64

11.  $3.94
    +$2.75

12.  $8.56
    +$4.03

13.  $9.08
    +$1.98

14.  $5.00
    −$3.59

15.  $4.50
    −$1.29

16.  $10.00
    − $ 5.20

## Mixed Review

Write the missing number.

17. _____ tens = 50

18. _____ hundreds = 300

19. _____ tens = 90

20. _____ thousands = 6,000

21. _____ dimes = 4 quarters

22. 15 pennies = _____ dimes

_____ pennies

23. 12 dimes = _____ dollars

_____ dimes

24. 8 dimes = _____ quarters

_____ dimes

25. 26 nickels = _____ dollars

_____ dimes

26. 15 dimes = _____ dollars

_____ quarters

# Time to the Minute

Read and write each time.

1.

2.

3.

_____

_____

_____

4.

5.

6.

_____

_____

_____

7.

8.

9.

_____

_____

_____

## Mixed Review

| 10. | 632 | 11. | 552 | 12. | 139 | 13. | 2,345 |
| | 421 | | 773 | | 777 | | 1,827 |
| | +267 | | +804 | | +609 | | + 4,558 |

| 14. | $57.90 | 15. | 4,414 | 16. | $15.99 | 17. | 7,212 |
| | −$39.00 | | −3,399 | | +$33.75 | | −3,946 |

Name _____

# A.M. and P.M.

Write the time, using A.M. or P.M.

1. still sleeping

_____

2. dentist appointment

_____

3. paint a picture

_____

4. lunch time

_____

5. the sunrise

_____

6. this a new day

_____

7. this day is almost over

_____

8. do the dishes

_____

9. eat breakfast

_____

## Mixed Review

Write + or − to make the sentence true.

10. 36 ◯ 27 = 9

11. 16 = 14 ◯ 2

12. 35 ◯ 18 = 53

13. 15 = 22 ◯ 7

Subtract.

14. $1.68
   −$0.09

15. $5.62
   −$3.17

16. $8.13
   −$3.59

17. $12.72
   −$ 7.49

# Elapsed Time

Use a clock to find the elapsed time.

**1.** start: 4:15 P.M.
end: 4:30 P.M.

_____

**2.** start: 5:30 P.M.
end: 5:45 P.M.

_____

**3.** start: 3:30 A.M.
end: 4:15 A.M.

_____

Use a clock to find the end time.

**4.** starting time: 4:15 P.M.
elapsed time: 30 minutes

_____

**5.** starting time: 2:00 A.M.
elapsed time: 1 hour and
30 minutes

_____

**6.** starting time: 7:30 A.M.
elapsed time: 45 minutes

_____

**7.** starting time: 3:45 P.M.
elapsed time: 15 minutes

_____

# Mixed Review

Write $<$, $>$, or $=$ in each $\bigcirc$.

**8.** $1{,}980 - 1{,}298 \bigcirc 682$

**9.** $782 + 886 \bigcirc 312 + 552$

**10.** $\$6{,}887 + \$2{,}021 \bigcirc \$9{,}000$

**11.** $499 - 107 \bigcirc 307$

Write in standard form.

**12.** six thousand, three hundred forty-two _____

**13.** $10{,}000 + 5{,}000 + 900 + 30 + 2$ _____

**14.** $20{,}000 + 7{,}000 + 400 + 80 + 7$ _____

**15.** eighty-four thousand, thirty-three _____

# Use a Schedule

Complete the schedule.

| CAMP WINDY SCHEDULE | | | |
|---|---|---|---|
| | Activity | Time | Elapsed Time |
| 1. | tennis | 9:00 A.M. – 10:00 A.M. | 1 hour |
| 2. | snack | 10:00 A.M. – 10:25 A.M. | _____ |
| 3. | crafts | _____ – 11:30 A.M. | 1 hour 5 minutes |
| 4. | lunch | 11:30 A.M. – _____ | 45 minutes |
| 5. | reading and games | _____ – 1:00 P.M. | 45 minutes |
| 6. | swimming | 1:00 P.M. – 2:15 P.M. | _____ |

For 7–10, use the schedule you completed.

7. Which activity ends at 10:25 A.M.? 11:30 A.M.?

_____

8. Reading and games begins ____ minutes after lunch begins.

_____

9. Crafts ends ____ hours ____ minutes after 9:00 A.M.

_____

10. Which activity is the longest?

_____

## Mixed Review

Write the greatest number possible with these digits.

11. 3, 7, 1, 5 _____     12. 4, 1, 1, 5, 4 _____     13. 6, 7, 3, 8, 5 _____

Tell whether the number is *odd* or *even*.

14. 16 _____     15. 3,451 _____     16. 5,467 _____     17. 834 _____

Find 1,000 more.

18. 398 _____     19. 1,309 _____     20. 5,833 _____     21. 10 _____

Compare the numbers. Write $<$, $>$, or $=$ in each $\bigcirc$.

22. 56 $\bigcirc$ 29     23. 247 $\bigcirc$ 417     24. 702 $\bigcirc$ 702     25. 212 $\bigcirc$ 199

Name _____

LESSON 6.5

## Use a Calendar

For 1–4, use the calendars.

| January 2002 | | | | | | |
|---|---|---|---|---|---|---|
| Sun. | Mon. | Tue. | Wed. | Thu. | Fri. | Sat. |
| | 1 | 2 | 3 | 4 | 5 | 6 |
| 7 | 8 | 9 | 10 | 11 | 12 | 13 |
| 14 | 15 | 16 | 17 | 18 | 19 | 20 |
| 21 | 22 | 23 | 24 | 25 | 26 | 27 |
| 28 | 29 | 30 | 31 | | | |

| February 2002 | | | | | | |
|---|---|---|---|---|---|---|
| Sun. | Mon. | Tue. | Wed. | Thu. | Fri. | Sat. |
| | | | | 1 | 2 | 3 |
| 4 | 5 | 6 | 7 | 8 | 9 | 10 |
| 11 | 12 | 13 | 14 | 15 | 16 | 17 |
| 18 | 19 | 20 | 21 | 22 | 23 | 24 |
| 25 | 26 | 27 | 28 | | | |

| March 2002 | | | | | | |
|---|---|---|---|---|---|---|
| Sun. | Mon. | Tue. | Wed. | Thu. | Fri. | Sat. |
| | | | | 1 | 2 | 3 |
| 4 | 5 | 6 | 7 | 8 | 9 | 10 |
| 11 | 12 | 13 | 14 | 15 | 16 | 17 |
| 18 | 19 | 20 | 21 | 22 | 23 | 24 |
| 25 | 26 | 27 | 28 | 29 | 30 | 31 |

1. The Youngs are leaving on January 1 and will be away for 3 weeks and 4 days. When will they return?

_____

2. Jamie left for a 2-week trip on February 26. She came home for two weeks and then left again for 6 days. Did she return on March 30? Explain.

_____

3. Tom is feeding a cat from February 6 to February 20. How many days is he feeding it? How many weeks?

_____

4. Tom is keeping Becky's hamsters at his house from March 13 to March 20. How many days is he keeping the hamsters? How many weeks?

_____

5. How many days is 2 weeks and 1 day?

_____

6. Eighteen days is _____ weeks and _____ days.

## Mixed Review

Round each number to the nearest thousand.

7. 3,714 _____

8. 5,901 _____

9. 6,379 _____

10. Write 3,072 in word form. _____

11. Write 531 in word form. _____

© Harcourt

Practice   PW33

# Problem Solving Skill

## Sequence Events

For 1–4, use the calendars and the list.

| September 2002 |
| --- |

| Sun. | Mon. | Tue. | Wed. | Thu. | Fri. | Sat. |
| --- | --- | --- | --- | --- | --- | --- |
| 1 | 2 | 3 | 4 | 5 | 6 | 7 |
| 8 | 9 | 10 | 11 | 12 | 13 | 14 |
| 15 | 16 | 17 | 18 | 19 | 20 | 21 |
| 22 | 23 | 24 | 25 | 26 | 27 | 28 |
| 29 | 30 | | | | | |

| October 2002 |
| --- |

| Sun. | Mon. | Tue. | Wed. | Thu. | Fri. | Sat. |
| --- | --- | --- | --- | --- | --- | --- |
| | | 1 | 2 | 3 | 4 | 5 |
| 6 | 7 | 8 | 9 | 10 | 11 | 12 |
| 13 | 14 | 15 | 16 | 17 | 18 | 19 |
| 20 | 21 | 22 | 23 | 24 | 25 | 26 |
| 27 | 28 | 29 | 30 | 31 | | |

| Today's date: September 9 |
| --- |
| Date of hay ride: October 13 |
| **Things to do:** |
| • Rent hay wagon 3 weeks before hay ride. |
| • Send invitations in 8 days. |
| • Order food 3 days before hay ride. |

1. Use the list of things to do to help plan a hay ride. Write what needs to be done in order and include the date for each.

_____

_____

_____

2. What if today's date is September 17 and the date of the hay ride changes to October 21? Write what needs to be done in order and include the date for each.

_____

_____

_____

3. Loni leaves on September 16 and will be gone for 11 days. She wants to cancel her paper delivery 1 week before she leaves and start it again the day she returns. What should she tell her paper girl?

_____

_____

4. Max has been invited to go on the hay ride. He will be out of town for 17 days beginning on September 25. Will he be home in time to go on the hay ride on October 13?

_____

_____

## Mixed Review

5. $175 + \underline{\quad} = 675$  6. $60 - \underline{\quad} = 35$  7. $237 + \underline{\quad} = 981$

# Algebra: Connect Addition and Multiplication

For 1–4, choose the letter of the number sentence that matches.

1. $6 + 6 + 6 + 6 + 6 = 30$ _____

2. $4 + 4 + 4 + 4 + 4 + 4 + 4 + 4 = 32$ _____

3. $5 + 5 + 5 + 5 = 20$ _____

4. $2 + 2 + 2 + 2 + 2 + 2 + 2 + 2 + 2 + 2 = 20$ _____

A $8 \times 4 = 32$

B $10 \times 2 = 20$

C $5 \times 6 = 30$

D $4 \times 5 = 20$

For 5–22, find the total. You may wish to draw a picture.

5. 2 groups of 6 = ___     6. 3 groups of 5 = ___     7. 2 groups of 4 = ___

8. 5 groups of 2 = ___     9. 6 groups of 3 = ___     10. 7 groups of 3 = ___

11. $3 + 3 + 3 + 3 =$ ___     12. $6 + 6 + 6 =$ ___     13. $8 + 8 =$ ___

14. $5 + 5 + 5 + 5 + 5$ = ___     15. $2 + 2 + 2 + 2$ = ___     16. $1 + 1 + 1 + 1 + 1 + 1$ = ___

17. $6 \times 1 =$ ___     18. $3 \times 2 =$ ___     19. $2 \times 9 =$ ___

20. $7 \times 2 =$ ___     21. $1 \times 7 =$ ___     22. $5 \times 5 =$ ___

## Mixed Review

Write the missing number that makes the sentence true.

23. $4 + \square = 16$   24. $5 = \square - 3$   25. $\square + 16 = 22$   26. $130 = 100 + \square$

27. $\square + 7 = 23$   28. $12 + \square = 30$   29. $15 = \square + 2$   30. $70 + \square = 85$

Add.

31.  $\begin{array}{r} 28 \\ + 17 \\ \hline \end{array}$   32.  $\begin{array}{r} 156 \\ + 813 \\ \hline \end{array}$   33.  $\begin{array}{r} 1{,}608 \\ + 1{,}097 \\ \hline \end{array}$   34.  $\begin{array}{r} 3{,}499 \\ + 3{,}499 \\ \hline \end{array}$

35.  $\begin{array}{r} 362 \\ + 412 \\ \hline \end{array}$   36.  $\begin{array}{r} 2{,}130 \\ + 9{,}805 \\ \hline \end{array}$   37.  $\begin{array}{r} 4{,}091 \\ + 1{,}904 \\ \hline \end{array}$   38.  $\begin{array}{r} 2{,}694 \\ + 1{,}739 \\ \hline \end{array}$

# Multiply with 2 and 5

## Vocabulary

Circle the word that best completes each sentence.

1. (Factors, Products) are numbers that you multiply.

2. The answer to a multiplication problem is the
   (factor, product).

---

Find the product.

3. (♠♠♠♠♠) (♠♠♠♠♠)
   (♠♠♠♠♠)

   $3 \times 5 =$ _____

4. (⚽⚽)(⚽⚽)(⚽⚽)
   (⚽⚽)(⚽⚽)

   $5 \times 2 =$ _____

5. (XXXXXXXXX)
   (XXXXXXXXX)

   $2 \times 9 =$ _____

6. (JJJJJJ) (JJJJJJ)
   (JJJJJJ) (JJJJJJ)
   (JJJJJJ)

   $5 \times 6 =$ _____

7. (KK) (KK) (KK)

   $3 \times 2 =$ _____

Complete.

8. $7 \times 5 =$ _____

9. _____ $= 3 \times 2$

10. $8 \times 5 =$ _____

11. _____ $= 2 \times 2$

12. $9 \times 5 =$ _____

13. $2 \times 5 =$ _____

14. $5 \times 6 =$ _____

15. $8 \times 2 =$ _____

## Mixed Review

16. $13 + 34 + 45 =$ _____

17. $8,237 - 3,389 =$ _____

18. $\$5.67$
    $+ \$3.57$

19. $\$20.72$
    $+ \$14.98$

20. $\$28.36$
    $+ \$ 1.70$

21. $\$52.80$
    $+ \$19.55$

22. Round 6,889 to the nearest
    hundred.

    _____

23. The elapsed time from
    3:15 P.M. to 5:15 P.M. is __?__.

    **A** 15 minutes     **C** two hours

    **B** one hour     **D** five hours

Name _____

# Arrays

Draw an array for each.

**1.**

3 rows of 2 = 6

**2.**

4 rows of 5 = 20

**3.**

2 rows of 6 = 12

**4.**

$4 \times 2 = 8$

**5.**

$4 \times 6 = 24$

**6.**

$6 \times 3 = 18$

Find the product. You may wish to draw an array.

**7.** $6 \times 2 =$ ___    **8.** $5 \times 2 =$ ___    **9.** $2 \times 7 =$ ___

**10.** $5 \times 5 =$ ___    **11.** $1 \times 4 =$ ___    **12.** $9 \times 3 =$ ___

## Mixed Review

Write the missing number that makes the sentence true.

**13.** $34 - \boxed{\phantom{00}} = 26$    **14.** $\boxed{\phantom{00}} - 12 = 28$

**15.** $\boxed{\phantom{00}} + 53 = 82$    **16.** $98 + 102 = \boxed{\phantom{00}}$

Add.

| **17.** | **18.** | **19.** | **20.** |
|---|---|---|---|
| 132 | 458 | 722 | 537 |
| 132 | 458 | 722 | 537 |
| + 132 | + 458 | + 722 | + 537 |

| **21.** | **22.** | **23.** | **24.** |
|---|---|---|---|
| 281 | 76 | 2,521 | 3,715 |
| 821 | 75 | 6,642 | 6,142 |
| + 128 | + 74 | + 7,908 | + 4,143 |

# Multiply with 3

Use the number line to find the product.

1. $5 \times 3 =$ _____
2. $3 \times 5 =$ _____

3. $5 \times 5 =$ _____
4. $4 \times 3 =$ _____
5. $9 \times 3 =$ _____
6. $2 \times 3 =$ _____

7. $4 \times 5 =$ _____
8. $3 \times 8 =$ _____
9. $7 \times 2 =$ _____
10. $3 \times 3 =$ _____

11. $9 \times 5 =$ _____
12. $6 \times 3 =$ _____
13. $2 \times 2 =$ _____
14. $5 \times 3 =$ _____

15. $8 \times 2 =$ _____
16. $5 \times 9 =$ _____
17. $2 \times 9 =$ _____
18. $6 \times 5 =$ _____

19. $5 \times 4 =$ _____
20. $3 \times 9 =$ _____
21. $5 \times 2 =$ _____
22. $7 \times 3 =$ _____

23. $8 \times 5 =$ _____
24. $7 \times 5 =$ _____
25. $2 \times 5 =$ _____

26. $5 \times 8 =$ _____
27. $3 \times 4 =$ _____
28. $2 \times 7 =$ _____

29. $3 \times 6 =$ _____
30. $9 \times 2 =$ _____
31. $8 \times 4 =$ _____

## Mixed Review

Circle the letter for the correct answer.

32. $24 + 56 + 12 =$ ▓

   A 29      C 101

   B 82      D 92

33. $17 + 11 + 45 =$ ▓

   F 53      H 84

   G 73      J 102

34. $12 + 9 + 19 =$ ▓

   A 40      C 45

   B 42      D 49

35. $62 + 15 + 27 =$ ▓

   F 88      H 104

   G 92      J 114

36. $25 + 35 + 45 =$ ▓

   A 75      C 90

   B 85      D 105

37. $26 + 38 + 7 =$ ▓

   F 69      H 78

   G 71      J 81

# Problem Solving Skill

## Too Much/Too Little Information

| Garden Supplies | |
|---|---|
| hoe | $9 |
| rake | $8 |
| package of seeds | $2 |

For 1–6, use the table.

For 1–4, write *a, b,* or *c* to tell whether the problem has *a.* too much information, *b.* too little information, or *c.* the right amount of information. Solve those with too much or the right amount of information.

**1.** Mario bought 2 rakes. He was in the garden store 15 minutes. How much did Mario spend?

_____

**2.** Cecil left at 5:00 P.M. to go to the garden store. He spent more on seeds than he did on other garden supplies. How much did he spend on seeds?

_____

**3.** Jerome had $20. He bought 7 packages of seeds. How much did he spend?

_____

**4.** Elaine had $20. She bought one hoe and two shovels. How much did she spend?

_____

**5.** You have $25 to spend on garden supplies. Which items can you buy?

  **A** 2 hoes, 2 rakes

  **B** 3 rakes, a package of seeds

  **C** 2 hoes, 4 packages of seeds

  **D** a hoe, 2 rakes

**6.** You have $30. How much more money do you need if you choose to buy 4 packages of seeds, 2 rakes and 2 hoes?

  **F** $42          **H** $12

  **G** $13          **J** $10

## Mixed Review

Write the time.

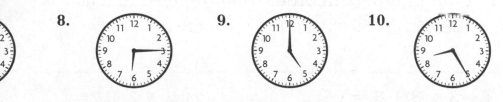

**7.**      **8.**      **9.**      **10.**

_____  _____  _____  _____

**11.** Are the hours between midnight and noon A.M. or P.M.? _____

# Multiply with 0 and 1

Complete the multiplication sentence to show the number of sneakers.

 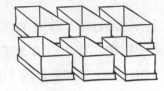 

**1.** $3 \times 1 =$ _____　　　　**2.** $6 \times 0 =$ _____　　　　**3.** $1 \times 2 =$ _____

Find the product.

**4.** $8 \times 0 =$ _____　　**5.** $1 \times 6 =$ _____　　**6.** $0 \times 5 =$ _____　　**7.** $9 \times 1 =$ _____

**8.** $1 \times 4 =$ _____　　**9.** $0 \times 3 =$ _____　　**10.** $1 \times 8 =$ _____　　**11.** $0 \times 1 =$ _____

**12.** $0 \times 0 =$ _____　　**13.** $5 \times 1 =$ _____　　**14.** $7 \times 0 =$ _____　　**15.** $2 \times 5 =$ _____

**16.** $5 \times 4 =$ _____　　**17.** $6 \times 3 =$ _____　　**18.** $3 \times 7 =$ _____　　**19.** $8 \times 2 =$ _____

## Mixed Review

**20.** Find the value of the bold digit.

43,9**7**5 _____　　　　78,**2**14 _____

**9**0,255 _____　　　　33,4**3**6 _____

29,**4**67 _____　　　　89,**6**12 _____

**21.** Find the sum of 198 and 864. _____

**22.** Put the numbers in order from least to greatest.

74　　　　44　　　　62　　　　47

_____

**23.** Put the numbers in order from greatest to least.

29　　　　59　　　　13　　　　68

_____

**24.** $3 + 3 + 3 + 3 =$ _____　　　　**25.** $2 + 2 + 2 =$ _____

Name _____

# Multiply with 4

Find the product.

1.  $\begin{array}{r} 4 \\ \times 4 \\ \hline \end{array}$
2.  $\begin{array}{r} 1 \\ \times 4 \\ \hline \end{array}$
3.  $\begin{array}{r} 4 \\ \times 7 \\ \hline \end{array}$
4.  $\begin{array}{r} 9 \\ \times 4 \\ \hline \end{array}$
5.  $\begin{array}{r} 4 \\ \times 3 \\ \hline \end{array}$
6.  $\begin{array}{r} 2 \\ \times 4 \\ \hline \end{array}$
7.  $\begin{array}{r} 4 \\ \times 8 \\ \hline \end{array}$

8.  $\begin{array}{r} 0 \\ \times 4 \\ \hline \end{array}$
9.  $\begin{array}{r} 5 \\ \times 4 \\ \hline \end{array}$
10.  $\begin{array}{r} 3 \\ \times 2 \\ \hline \end{array}$
11.  $\begin{array}{r} 2 \\ \times 4 \\ \hline \end{array}$
12.  $\begin{array}{r} 1 \\ \times 4 \\ \hline \end{array}$
13.  $\begin{array}{r} 7 \\ \times 3 \\ \hline \end{array}$
14.  $\begin{array}{r} 9 \\ \times 2 \\ \hline \end{array}$

15.  $\begin{array}{r} 8 \\ \times 2 \\ \hline \end{array}$
16.  $\begin{array}{r} 3 \\ \times 5 \\ \hline \end{array}$
17.  $\begin{array}{r} 5 \\ \times 1 \\ \hline \end{array}$
18.  $\begin{array}{r} 6 \\ \times 5 \\ \hline \end{array}$
19.  $\begin{array}{r} 0 \\ \times 3 \\ \hline \end{array}$
20.  $\begin{array}{r} 1 \\ \times 2 \\ \hline \end{array}$
21.  $\begin{array}{r} 7 \\ \times 0 \\ \hline \end{array}$

22. $4 \times 6 =$ _____
23. $1 \times 0 =$ _____
24. $5 \times 3 =$ _____
25. $0 \times 9 =$ _____

26. $4 \times 0 =$ _____
27. $5 \times 4 =$ _____
28. $1 \times 0 =$ _____
29. $8 \times 3 =$ _____

## Mixed Review

30.  $\begin{array}{r} \$6.27 \\ +\$2.66 \\ \hline \end{array}$
31.  $\begin{array}{r} \$7.99 \\ -\$4.44 \\ \hline \end{array}$
32.  $\begin{array}{r} \$8.31 \\ -\$5.98 \\ \hline \end{array}$
33.  $\begin{array}{r} \$2.28 \\ +\$7.95 \\ \hline \end{array}$

34. $305 + 882 + 406 =$ _____
35. $761 + 75 =$ _____

36. Which shows the numbers in order from least to greatest?

  A 786    867    678

  B 867    678    786

  C 678    786    867

What is the value of the 4 in each of these numbers?

37. 9,412      38. 24      39. 46,118

_____    _____    _____

©Harcourt

# Problem Solving Strategy

## Find a Pattern

Use *find a pattern* to solve.

1. Quintin's pattern is 2, 5, 8, 11, 14, and 17. What is the rule? What are the next four numbers in his pattern?

_____

2. Vernon's pattern is 12, 15, 19, 22, and 26. What is the rule? What are the next four numbers in his pattern?

_____

3. Laura's pattern is 14, 24, 34, 44, and 54. What is the rule? What are the next four numbers in her pattern?

_____

4. Marianne's pattern is 31, 36, 41, 46, and 51. What is the rule? What are the next four numbers in her pattern?

_____

5. Sharon's pattern is 54, 51, 48, 45, 42, and 39. What is the rule? What are the next four numbers in her pattern?

_____

6. Tom's pattern is 10, 12, 13, 15, 16, and 18. What is the rule? What are the next four numbers in his pattern?

_____

7. Myrone's pattern is 1, 5, 9, 13, 17, and 21. What is the rule? What are the next four numbers in his pattern?

_____

8. Melinda's pattern is 9, 7, 10, 8, 11, 9, and 12. What is the rule? What are the next four numbers in her pattern?

_____

## Mixed Review

Round to the nearest ten thousands.

9. 127,803 _____  10. 199,975 _____  11. 259,099 _____

Write >, <, or =.

12. $5.67 _____ $5.76   13. $16.10 _____ $16.09  14. $4.89 _____ $4.90

Find 100 more than the number.

15. 2,376 _____   16. 45,903 _____   17. 119,752 _____

# Practice Multiplication

Complete the tables.

**1.**

| × | 3 | 6 | 7 | 2 | 5 |
|---|---|---|---|---|---|
| 4 |   |   |   |   |   |

**2.**

| × | 5 | 4 | 6 | 7 | 8 |
|---|---|---|---|---|---|
| 5 |   |   |   |   |   |

**3.**

| × | 6 | 7 | 8 | 3 | 5 |
|---|---|---|---|---|---|
| 3 |   |   |   |   |   |

**4.**

| × | 8 | 2 | 4 | 3 | 6 |
|---|---|---|---|---|---|
| 2 |   |   |   |   |   |

Find the product.

**5.** $1 \times 6 =$ _____

**6.** $2 \times 8 =$ _____

**7.** $2 \times 7 =$ _____

**8.** $4 \times 8 =$ _____

**9.** $3 \times 7 =$ _____

**10.** $4 \times 2 =$ _____

**11.** $8 \times 3 =$ _____

**12.** $4 \times 6 =$ _____

**13.** $2 \times 9 =$ _____

**14.** $4 \times 1 =$ _____

**15.** $5 \times 5 =$ _____

**16.** $1 \times 3 =$ _____

## Mixed Review

**17.** How many minutes are between 11:30 P.M. and

11:45 P.M.? _____

**18.** $5.98
      +$2.07

**19.**    702
        − 67

**20.** $ 0.71
       +$10.49

**21.**   6,498
        − 3,512

**22.** _____ $+ 21 = 29$

**23.** $72 - 33 =$ _____

**24.** $923 + 765 =$ _____

**25.** $4,099 - 170 =$ _____

**26.** Which shows the numbers in order from greatest to least?

    **A** 789    897    987

    **B** 987    897    789

    **C** 897    987    789

# Algebra: Find Missing Factors

Find the missing factor.

1. ____ × 4 = 20          2. 7 × ____ = 35          3. ____ × 6 = 18

4. 8 × ____ = 32          5. ____ × 3 = 27          6. 5 × ____ = 30

7. ____ × 5 = 15          8. ____ × 3 = 21          9. 8 × ____ = 24

10. 5 × ____ = 25          11. ____ × 4 = 24          12. ____ × 4 = 36

13. ____ × 4 = 32          14. 4 × ____ = 20          15. 2 × ____ = 12

16. 5 × ____ = 45          17. 8 × ____ = 24          18. ____ × 2 = 10

19. 3 × ____ = 27          20. ____ × 3 = 3          21. 4 × ____ = 16

22. 7 × ____ = 2 × ____          23. 5 × ____ = 45 − 5

## Mixed Review

Add 8 to each.

24. 42          25. 216          26. 181          27. 437

_____          _____          _____          _____

Write the total value of each.

28. 2 dimes          29. 3 quarters          30. 3 $1-bills          31. 2 $1-bills
    3 nickels             5 nickels               4 quarters            2 quarters
    4 pennies            8 pennies               10 dimes              2 dimes

_____          _____          _____          _____

32. $17.25 + $6.00 = _____          33. $0.79 + $0.40 + $0.88 = _____

Complete the tables.

34.

| × | 9 | 5 | 1 | 4 | 6 |
|---|---|---|---|---|---|
| 2 |   |   |   |   |   |

35.

| × | 4 | 0 | 3 | 8 | 7 |
|---|---|---|---|---|---|
| 0 |   |   |   |   |   |

Name _____

**Find each product.**

2. $4 \times 6 =$ _____   3. $3 \times 8 =$ _____   4. $6 \times 2 =$ _____

5. $5 \times 4 =$ _____   6. $8 \times 6 =$ _____   7. $6 \times 5 =$ _____

8. $7 \times 6 =$ _____   9. $3 \times 9 =$ _____   10. $6 \times 6 =$ _____

11. $6 \times 0 =$ _____   12. $1 \times 6 =$ _____   13. $4 \times 9 =$ _____

14. $\begin{array}{r} 9 \\ \times 6 \\ \hline \end{array}$   15. $\begin{array}{r} 7 \\ \times 4 \\ \hline \end{array}$   16. $\begin{array}{r} 6 \\ \times 3 \\ \hline \end{array}$   17. $\begin{array}{r} 3 \\ \times 4 \\ \hline \end{array}$

**Complete the multiplication table.**

18.

| × | 1 | 2 | 3 | 4 | 5 | 6 | 7 | 8 | 9 |
|---|---|---|---|---|---|---|---|---|---|
| 6 | ___ | ___ | ___ | ___ | ___ | ___ | ___ | ___ | ___ |

**Mixed Review**

Solve.

19. $\begin{array}{r} 4,009 \\ -2,389 \\ \hline \end{array}$   20. $\begin{array}{r} 387 \\ +906 \\ \hline \end{array}$   21. $\begin{array}{r} \$62.85 \\ -\$34.99 \\ \hline \end{array}$   22. $\begin{array}{r} 1,709 \\ +5,913 \\ \hline \end{array}$

23. $\begin{array}{r} \$5.49 \\ +\$3.89 \\ \hline \end{array}$   24. $\begin{array}{r} 7,360 \\ -2,507 \\ \hline \end{array}$   25. $\begin{array}{r} 6,906 \\ -6,079 \\ \hline \end{array}$   26. $\begin{array}{r} \$4,788 \\ +\$\ \ 613 \\ \hline \end{array}$

# Multiply with 7

Find each product.

1. $7 \times 6 =$ _____    2. $5 \times 2 =$ _____    3. $3 \times 7 =$ _____

4. $7 \times 4 =$ _____    5. $6 \times 7 =$ _____    6. $4 \times 8 =$ _____

7. $9 \times 7 =$ _____    8. $5 \times 1 =$ _____    9. $7 \times 0 =$ _____

10. $1 \times 7 =$ _____    11. $7 \times 5 =$ _____    12. $7 \times 2 =$ _____

Complete the multiplication table.

13.

| × | 1 | 2 | 3 | 4 | 5 | 6 | 7 | 8 | 9 |
|---|---|---|---|---|---|---|---|---|---|
| 7 | ___ | ___ | ___ | ___ | ___ | ___ | ___ | ___ | ___ |

Complete.

14. $9 \times 7 =$ ____ $+ 33$    15. $7 \times$ ____ $= 34 - 13$    16. ____ $\times 7 = 7 + 7$

## Mixed Review

Write the value of the underlined digit.

17. 53,009 _____    18. 6,842 _____    19. 92,106 _____

20. 4,222 _____    21. 11,001 _____    22. 6,681 _____

Round to the nearest hundred.

23. 5,349 _____    24. 478 _____    25. 14,780 _____

26. 26,318 _____    27. 1,159 _____    28. 879 _____

Subtract 475 from each number.

29. 690    30. 4,330    31. 2,065

_____    _____    _____

32. 1,010    33. 17,342    34. 9,999

_____    _____    _____

Name _____

# Multiply with 8

Find each product.

1. $4 \times 8 = $ _____   2. $8 \times 7 = $ _____   3. $4 \times 6 = $ _____

4. $3 \times 8 = $ _____   5. $8 \times 9 = $ _____   6. $6 \times 7 = $ _____

7. $8 \times 0 = $ _____   8. $2 \times 8 = $ _____   9. $5 \times 8 = $ _____

10.  $\begin{array}{r} 7 \\ \times 2 \\ \hline \end{array}$   11.  $\begin{array}{r} 1 \\ \times 8 \\ \hline \end{array}$   12.  $\begin{array}{r} 8 \\ \times 6 \\ \hline \end{array}$   13.  $\begin{array}{r} 8 \\ \times 8 \\ \hline \end{array}$

Complete the multiplication table.

14.

| × | 1 | 2 | 3 | 4 | 5 | 6 | 7 | 8 | 9 |
|---|---|---|---|---|---|---|---|---|---|
| 8 | ___ | ___ | ___ | ___ | ___ | ___ | ___ | ___ | ___ |

Compare. Write $<$, $>$, or $=$ in each ◯.

15. $8 \times 4$ ◯ $2 \times 6$   16. $8 \times 3$ ◯ $6 \times 8$

17. $7 \times 0$ ◯ $8 \times 0$   18. $4 \times 5$ ◯ $6 \times 7$

19. $8 \times 9$ ◯ $3 \times 4$   20. $5 \times 5$ ◯ $8 \times 8$

## Mixed Review

Solve.

21. $32 + 44 + 81 = $ _____   22. $56 + 14 + 39 = $ _____

23. $82 + 8 + 18 = $ _____   24. $28 + 27 + 42 = $ _____

25. $4{,}290 - 3{,}735 = $ _____   26. $10{,}802 - 6{,}529 = $ _____

27. $5{,}000 - 655 = $ _____   28. $3{,}800 - 799 = $ _____

# Problem Solving Strategy

## Draw a Picture

Use *draw a picture* to solve.

1. Mrs. King has 14 pictures. Name one way she can arrange them in equal rows.

2. Mr. Queen decides to arrange his 18 pictures in equal rows of 6. How many rows will he have?

_____

3. Kevin has 9 squares. How can he arrange them to form one large square?

4. Trisha has 36 squares. How can she arrange them to form one large square?

_____

5. Alan put 27 stickers in 3 equal rows. How many stickers did he put in each row?

6. June put 32 stickers in 4 equal rows. How many stickers did she put in each row?

_____

7. Wes baked cookies. He put 18 cookies on a cookie sheet. If he made 6 equal rows of cookies, how many cookies did he put in each row?

8. Patty baked cupcakes. She put 21 in a box. If she made 7 equal rows, how many cupcakes did she put in each row?

_____

## Mixed Review

Write how many there are in all.

9. 3 groups of 8      10. 7 groups of 4      11. 3 groups of 5

_____

Subtract.

12.
```
  1,609
-   854
```

13.
```
  4,000
- 2,450
```

14.
```
 15,830
- 9,622
```

15.
```
  6,317
- 4,719
```

© Harcourt

Name _____

# Algebra: Practice the Facts

Find each product.

1. $5 \times 4 =$ _____   2. $6 \times 6 =$ _____   3. $8 \times 6 =$ _____

4. $7 \times 7 =$ _____   5. $3 \times 5 =$ _____   6. $6 \times 9 =$ _____

7. $8 \times 9 =$ _____   8. $6 \times 7 =$ _____   9. $5 \times 6 =$ _____

10. $8 \times 5 =$ _____   11. $8 \times 7 =$ _____   12. $8 \times 8 =$ _____

13. $5 \times 7 =$ _____   14. $9 \times 7 =$ _____   15. $5 \times 9 =$ _____

16.  5   17.  8   18.  7   19.  7
  $\times 2$      $\times 4$      $\times 8$      $\times 6$

20.  9   21.  4   22.  9   23.  4
  $\times 8$      $\times 4$      $\times 3$      $\times 7$

Find each missing factor.

24. $5 \times$ _____ $= 45$   25. $9 \times$ _____ $= 36$   26. $8 \times$ _____ $= 16$

27. $3 \times$ _____ $= 27$   28. $7 \times$ _____ $= 63$   29. _____ $\times 8 = 24$

30. _____ $\times 6 = 54$   31. _____ $\times 4 = 28$   32. $6 \times$ _____ $= 24$

## Mixed Review

Add.

33.  45   34.  43   35.  44   36.  73
   16       57       55       64
  $+27$      $+87$      $+66$      46
                            $+11$

# Multiply with 9 and 10

Complete the table.

| 1. × | 1 | 2 | 3 | 4 | 5 | 6 | 7 | 8 | 9 |
|---|---|---|---|---|---|---|---|---|---|
| 9 | ___ | ___ | ___ | ___ | ___ | ___ | ___ | ___ | ___ |
| 10 | ___ | ___ | ___ | ___ | ___ | ___ | ___ | ___ | ___ |

Find the product.

2.  9
$\times$ 5

3.  10
$\times$ 9

4.  10
$\times$ 6

5.  10
$\times$ 8

6.  9
$\times$ 4

7.  9
$\times$ 6

8.  10
$\times$ 5

9.  10
$\times$ 3

10.  7
$\times$ 9

11.  10
$\times$ 2

12.  9
$\times$ 3

13.  10
$\times$ 4

14.  9
$\times$ 9

15.  10
$\times$ 7

16.  8
$\times$ 9

17. $8 \times 10 =$ _____

18. $9 \times 2 =$ _____

19. $1 \times 10 =$ _____

20. $1 \times 9 =$ _____

21. $9 \times 10 =$ _____

22. $9 \times 5 =$ _____

23. $10 \times 2 =$ _____

24. $10 \times 8 =$ _____

25. $9 \times 7 =$ _____

Find the missing factor.

26. $\square \times 8 = 0$

27. $\square \times 2 = 20$

28. $7 \times \square = 7$

29. $9 \times \square = 6 \times 3$

30. $5 \times 8 = \square \times 10$

31. $\square \times 9 = 6 \times 6$

## Mixed Review

Add or subtract.

32.  $8.09
   $-$3.55

33.  $7.00
   $-$6.99

34.  $5.55
   $4.44
   $+$3.33

35.  $1.29
   $1.39
   $+$1.49

# Algebra: Find a Rule

Write a rule for each table. Then complete the table.

1.

| Flutes | 2 | 3 | 4 | 5 | 6 |
|---|---|---|---|---|---|
| Trumpets | 6 | 9 | 12 | | |

Rule: _____

2.

| Cups | 1 | 2 | 3 | 4 | 5 | 6 |
|---|---|---|---|---|---|---|
| Ounces | 8 | 16 | 24 | | | |

Rule: _____

3.

| Plates | 5 | 6 | 7 | 8 | 9 | 10 |
|---|---|---|---|---|---|---|
| Bowls | 10 | 12 | 14 | 16 | | |

Rule: _____

4.

| Plants | 4 | 5 | 6 | 7 | 8 | 9 |
|---|---|---|---|---|---|---|
| Flowers | 24 | 30 | 36 | | | |

Rule: _____

5. Each box holds 4 toys. How many toys do 5 boxes hold?

| Boxes | 1 | 2 | | | |
|---|---|---|---|---|---|
| Toys | 4 | 8 | | | |

Rule: _____

6. Four shelves hold 36 toys. How many toys do 9 shelves hold?

| Shelves | 4 | 5 | 6 | | |
|---|---|---|---|---|---|
| Toys | 36 | 45 | | | |

Rule: _____

## Mixed Review

Find the elapsed time.

7. 7:00 P.M. to 8:30 P.M.

8. 4:00 A.M. to noon

9. 9:00 A.M. to 1:00 P.M.

10. 6:30 P.M. to 10:15 P.M.

Use mental math to find the sum.

| 11. | 52 | 12. | 17 | 13. | 51 | 14. | 19 |
|---|---|---|---|---|---|---|---|
| | 48 | | 13 | | 49 | | 21 |
| | 24 | | 16 | | 47 | | 15 |
| | + 26 | | + 14 | | + 53 | | + 15 |

# Algebra: Multiply with 3 Factors

Find each product.

**1.** $(3 \times 2) \times 3 =$ _____   **2.** $6 \times (4 \times 2) =$ _____   **3.** $(3 \times 3) \times 5 =$ _____

**4.** $(2 \times 2) \times 8 =$ _____   **5.** $(1 \times 4) \times 7 =$ _____   **6.** $4 \times (7 \times 1) =$ _____

**7.** $6 \times (0 \times 7) =$ _____   **8.** $(3 \times 3) \times 10 =$ _____   **9.** $(7 \times 1) \times 8 =$ _____

Use the Grouping Property to find the product.

**10.** $3 \times 3 \times 6 =$ _____   **11.** $4 \times 4 \times 2 =$ _____   **12.** $9 \times 3 \times 2 =$ _____

**13.** $7 \times 2 \times 2 =$ _____   **14.** $(2 \times 4) \times 7 =$ _____   **15.** $4 \times (9 \times 1) =$ _____

**16.** $4 \times 2 \times 5 =$ _____   **17.** $(3 \times 2) \times 10 =$ _____   **18.** $4 \times 2 \times 7 =$ _____

Find the missing factor.

**19.** $(8 \times$ _____$) \times 8 = 0$   **20.** _____ $\times (3 \times 2) = 36$   **21.** $($_____ $\times 4) \times 3 = 12$

**22.** $6 \times (3 \times$ _____$) = 54$   **23.** $(3 \times 3) \times$ _____ $= 90$   **24.** _____ $\times (5 \times 2) = 80$

**25.** $($_____ $\times 1) \times 1 = 6$   **26.** $4 \times ($_____ $\times 4) = 32$   **27.** $(2 \times 4) \times$ _____ $= 64$

## Mixed Review

Write the missing number that makes each sentence true.

**28.** $9 +$ _____ $= 20$   **29.** $8 =$ _____ $- 3$

**30.** _____ $+ 13 = 44$   **31.** $560 = 200 +$ _____

Write $<$, $>$, or $=$ for each $\bigcirc$.

**32.** $544 \bigcirc 544$   **33.** $5,106 \bigcirc 5,099$   **34.** $467 + 3 \bigcirc 471$

Continue the pattern.

**35.** 6, 12, 18, 24, _____, _____, _____, _____

**36.** 39, 49, _____, 69, _____, _____, _____

**37.** 75, 70, 65, 60, 55, _____, _____, _____

# Problem Solving Skill
## Multistep Problems
Solve.

1. Taylor bought 6 used books that cost $2 each. He also bought 3 used books that cost $4 each. How much did Taylor spend on used books?

_____

2. Tina has 3 rows of 8 rocks in her rock collection. She wants to double her collection. How many rocks will Tina have when she doubles her collection?

_____

3. Howard has $138 and Tess has $149. They need a total of $250 to buy a recliner chair for their father. How much more money do they have than they need?

_____

4. To raise money for school, Megan sold 8 magazine subscriptions. Parker sold 7 subscriptions. Each subscription raises $5 for the school. How much money did they raise in all?

_____

5. The Romers drove 613 miles in 3 days. They drove 251 miles the first day and 168 miles the second day. How far did they drive on the third day?

_____

6. Two friends are comparing money. Bert has 8 quarters and 7 dimes. Ernie has 10 quarters and 7 nickels. Who has the most money? How much more money than his friend does he have?

_____

## Mixed Review
Continue the pattern.

7. 20, 40, 60, 80, _?_, _?_, _?_

8. 12, 14, 15, 17, 18, 20, _?_, _?_

Find the product.

9. $(2 \times 3) \times 9 =$ _____

10. $6 \times (3 \times 3) =$ _____

Name _____

# The Meaning of Division

Complete the table. Use counters to help.

|   | Counters | Number of equal groups | Number in each group |
|---|---|---|---|
| 1. | 10 | 2 | |
| 2. | 12 | | 6 |
| 3. | 16 | 4 | |
| 4. | 18 | | 6 |
| 5. | 21 | 3 | |

For 6–9, use counters.

6. Four family members want to share a bag of 20 pretzels equally. How many pretzels will each person get?

7. Carrie and two friends are sharing a pizza cut into 12 slices. If each person eats the same number of slices, how many slices will each person get?

8. Six students are sharing the job of watering the classroom plants. Each student waters 3 plants. How many plants are in the classroom altogether?

9. Emma's friends are helping her write a total of 16 invitations. Each person has 4 invitations to write. How many people are working together?

## Mixed Review

Solve.

10.  $77.42
    −$24.59

11.  3,071
    +  809

12.  468
    −312

13.  818
    −607

14.  6
    ×5

15.  8
    ×9

16.  7
    ×4

17.  3
    ×2

# Relate Subtraction and Division

Write a division sentence for each.

1.
$$\begin{array}{ccccc} 15 & 12 & 9 & 6 & 3 \\ -\ 3 & -\ 3 & -\ 3 & -\ 3 & -\ 3 \\ \hline 12 & 9 & 6 & 3 & 0 \end{array}$$

2.
$$\begin{array}{ccc} 18 & 12 & 6 \\ -\ 6 & -\ 6 & -\ 6 \\ \hline 12 & 6 & 0 \end{array}$$

_____

_____

3.
$$\begin{array}{ccccc} 10 & 8 & 6 & 4 & 2 \\ -\ 2 & -\ 2 & -\ 2 & -\ 2 & -\ 2 \\ \hline 8 & 6 & 4 & 2 & 0 \end{array}$$

4.
$$\begin{array}{cccc} 16 & 12 & 8 & 4 \\ -\ 4 & -\ 4 & -\ 4 & -\ 4 \\ \hline 12 & 8 & 4 & 0 \end{array}$$

_____

_____

Use subtraction to solve.

5. $12 \div 3 =$ _____

6. $20 \div 4 =$ _____

_____

_____

7. $30 \div 5 =$ _____

8. $6 \div 2 =$ _____

_____

_____

## Mixed Review

9.
$$\begin{array}{r} 271 \\ +409 \\ \hline \end{array}$$

10.
$$\begin{array}{r} 9,006 \\ -7,847 \\ \hline \end{array}$$

11.
$$\begin{array}{r} 7 \\ \times 6 \\ \hline \end{array}$$

12.
$$\begin{array}{r} 4 \\ \times 9 \\ \hline \end{array}$$

13. $7 \times 7 =$ _____

14. $8 \times 3 =$ _____

15. $8 \times 6 =$ _____

Name _____

# Algebra: Relate Multiplication and Division

Complete.

1.
4 rows of _____ = 20
20 ÷ 4 = _____

2.
3 rows of _____ = 21
21 ÷ 3 = _____

3.
4 rows of _____ = 36
36 ÷ 4 = _____

Complete each number sentence. Draw an array to help.

4. 6 × _____ = 18    5. 32 ÷ 8 = _____    6. 4 × 5 = _____

Complete.

7. 3 × 3 = 36 ÷ _____    8. _____ × 5 = 40 ÷ 4

## Mixed Review

9. 8 × 6 = _____    10. 4 × 9 = _____    11. 7 × 2 = _____

12. 760
−152

13. 3,789
+ 534

14. 8,117
−5,833

15. 6,211
−5,819

16. 380
+8,495

17. 7,117
+2,981

© Harcourt

# Algebra: Fact Families

Write the fact family.

1. 4, 9, 36

2. 8, 3, 24

3. 6, 4, 24

_____ _____ _____

_____ _____ _____

_____ _____ _____

_____ _____ _____

4. 6, 6, 36

5. 7, 7, 49

6. 5, 5, 25

_____ _____ _____

_____ _____ _____

Find the quotient or product.

7. $5 \times 7 =$ ____   8. $7 \times 5 =$ ____   9. $35 \div 7 =$ ____   10. $35 \div 5 =$ ____

Write the other three sentences in the fact family.

11. $6 \times 3 = 18$

12. $4 \times 5 = 20$

13. $2 \times 7 = 14$

_____ _____ _____

_____ _____ _____

_____ _____ _____

## Mixed Review

Write $+$, $-$, $\times$, or $\div$ in each $\bigcirc$.

14. $36 \bigcirc 4 = 9$

15. $18 \bigcirc 12 = 6$

16. $2 \bigcirc 8 = 16$

17. $72 \bigcirc 9 = 8$

18. $14 \bigcirc 4 = 10$

19. $9 \bigcirc 6 = 54$

# Problem Solving Strategy

## Write a Number Sentence

Write a number sentence to solve.

1. Mrs. Scott bought 3 packages of hot dogs. Each package has 8 hot dogs. How many hot dogs did she buy in all?

   _____

2. A class of 27 students is working in groups of 3 on an art project. How many groups are there?

   _____

3. Melissa took 24 photographs. She put 4 photographs on each page of her album. How many pages did she use?

   _____

4. Tim planted 5 rows of corn. There are 6 corn plants in each row. How many corn plants are there in all?

   _____

## Mixed Review

5.  $2.42
    +$5.65

6.  $4.91
    −$0.76

7.  $8.56
    −$3.28

8.  $7.99
    +$1.99

9.   8
    × 5

10.  5
    × 8

11.  9
    × 9

12.  6
    × 8

13. $3 \times 7 =$ _____

14. $6 \times 9 =$ _____

15. $10 \times 4 =$ _____

16. $4 \times 7 =$ _____

Write $+$, $-$, $\times$, or $\div$ in each $\bigcirc$.

17. $84 \bigcirc 25 = 59$

18. $6 \bigcirc 8 = 48$

19. $32 \bigcirc 73 = 105$

20. $54 \bigcirc 9 = 63$

21. $7 \bigcirc 6 = 42$

22. $9 \bigcirc 5 = 45$

© Harcourt

# Divide by 2 and 5

Find each missing factor and quotient.

1. $2 \times$ _____ $= 8$      2. $30 \div 5 =$ _____      3. $16 \div 2 =$ _____

4. $45 \div 5 =$ _____      5. $5 \times$ _____ $= 25$      6. $8 \div 2 =$ _____

7. $5 \times$ _____ $= 15$      8. $2 \times$ _____ $= 20$      9. $2 \times$ _____ $= 12$

Find each quotient.

10. $18 \div 2 =$ _____      11. $35 \div 5 =$ _____      12. $40 \div 5 =$ _____

13. $4 \div 2 =$ _____      14. $10 \div 2 =$ _____      15. $5 \div 5 =$ _____

16. $5\overline{)30}$      17. $2\overline{)14}$      18. $5\overline{)20}$      19. $5\overline{)5}$

20. $2\overline{)12}$      21. $2\overline{)8}$      22. $5\overline{)15}$      23. $5\overline{)40}$

Complete.

24. $20 \div 2 =$ _____      25. $15 \div 5 =$ _____ $\times 1$   26. $40 \div 5 =$ _____ $\times 2$

## Mixed Review

27. $9 \times 3 \times$ _____ $= 81$  28. _____ $\times 6 \times 2 = 12$   29. $9 \times$ _____ $= 63$

Add 1,000 to each.

30. $32,605$      31. $20,001$      32. $518$      33. $6$

_____  _____  _____  _____

Write A.M. or P.M.

34. ten minutes after midnight   35. time to go to bed   36. ten minutes before noon   37. ten minutes before midnight

_____  _____  _____  _____

# Divide by 3 and 4

Write the multiplication fact you can use to find the quotient. Then write the quotient.

**1.** $36 \div 4$

**2.** $21 \div 3$

**3.** $28 \div 4$

_____

_____

_____

_____

_____

_____

Find each quotient.

**4.** $18 \div 3 =$ _____

**5.** $32 \div 4 =$ _____

**6.** $30 \div 3 =$ _____

**7.** $8 \div 2 =$ _____

**8.** $12 \div 3 =$ _____

**9.** $12 \div 4 =$ _____

**10.** $3\overline{)15}$

**11.** $4\overline{)28}$

**12.** $3\overline{)27}$

**13.** $4\overline{)16}$

**14.** $4\overline{)32}$

**15.** $3\overline{)9}$

**16.** $4\overline{)8}$

**17.** $3\overline{)30}$

Complete.

**18.** $12 \div 4 =$ _____ $\times 3$    **19.** $24 \div 4 =$ _____ $\times 3$    **20.** $27 \div 3 =$ _____ $\times 3$

## Mixed Review

Solve.

**21.** $\begin{array}{r} 8 \\ \times 9 \\ \hline \end{array}$

**22.** $\begin{array}{r} 7 \\ \times 8 \\ \hline \end{array}$

**23.** $\begin{array}{r} 6 \\ \times 7 \\ \hline \end{array}$

**24.** $\begin{array}{r} 5 \\ \times 6 \\ \hline \end{array}$

**25.** $\begin{array}{r} 4 \\ \times 5 \\ \hline \end{array}$

**26.** $\begin{array}{r} 9 \\ \times 9 \\ \hline \end{array}$

**27.** $\begin{array}{r} 8 \\ \times 8 \\ \hline \end{array}$

**28.** $\begin{array}{r} 7 \\ \times 7 \\ \hline \end{array}$

**29.** $\begin{array}{r} 6 \\ \times 6 \\ \hline \end{array}$

**30.** $\begin{array}{r} 5 \\ \times 5 \\ \hline \end{array}$

**31.** $\begin{array}{r} \$13.87 \\ + \$25.62 \\ \hline \end{array}$

**32.** $\begin{array}{r} \$45.16 \\ + \$82.37 \\ \hline \end{array}$

**33.** $\begin{array}{r} \$63.27 \\ + \$37.92 \\ \hline \end{array}$

**34.** $\begin{array}{r} \$49.95 \\ + \$77.85 \\ \hline \end{array}$

# Divide with 0 and 1

Find each quotient.

1. $7 \div 7 =$ _____   2. $0 \div 5 =$ _____   3. $4 \div 1 =$ _____

4. $8 \div 1 =$ _____   5. $6 \div 6 =$ _____   6. $0 \div 3 =$ _____

7. $2 \div 2 =$ _____   8. $0 \div 8 =$ _____   9. $2 \div 1 =$ _____

10. $0 \div 4 =$ _____   11. $3 \div 1 =$ _____   12. $5 \div 5 =$ _____

13. $4 \div 4 =$ _____   14. $9 \div 1 =$ _____   15. $0 \div 2 =$ _____

16. $7 \div 1 =$ _____   17. $9 \div 9 =$ _____   18. $6 \div 1 =$ _____

19. $0 \div 1 =$ _____   20. $0 \div 9 =$ _____   21. $3 \div 3 =$ _____

Compare. Write $<$, $>$, or $=$ for each $\bigcirc$ .

22. $7 \div 7 \bigcirc 7 \div 1$   23. $9 \div 9 \bigcirc 10 - 9$   24. $5 \div 1 \bigcirc 5 + 1$

25. $0 \div 6 \bigcirc 6 + 0$   26. $2 + 4 \bigcirc 0 \div 6$   27. $3 \div 1 \bigcirc 3 \times 1$

## Mixed Review

28.  $\begin{array}{r} 475 \\ -352 \\ \hline \end{array}$   29.  $\begin{array}{r} 450 \\ +640 \\ \hline \end{array}$   30.  $\begin{array}{r} 7{,}991 \\ -4{,}328 \\ \hline \end{array}$   31.  $\begin{array}{r} 665 \\ +392 \\ \hline \end{array}$

32.  $\begin{array}{r} \$3.67 \\ +\$2.33 \\ \hline \end{array}$   33.  $\begin{array}{r} \$4.27 \\ +\$3.59 \\ \hline \end{array}$   34.  $\begin{array}{r} \$28.95 \\ -\$17.60 \\ \hline \end{array}$   35.  $\begin{array}{r} \$13.40 \\ -\$11.72 \\ \hline \end{array}$

Find each missing number.

36. $6 \div$ _____ $= 2$   37. $8 \div$ _____ $= 8$

38. _____ $\div 4 = 1$   39. _____ $\div 7 = 0$

# Write Expressions

Write an expression to describe each problem.

1. Kim has 18 craft sticks. His mother gives him 3 more. How many craft sticks does he have now?

   _____

2. Four students share 36 tacks. How many tacks does each student get?

   _____

3. Beth has a photo album with 9 pages. She can fit 8 photos on each page. How many photos can be put in the album?

   _____

4. Tim stacked 20 blocks. He then took away 8 of them. How many blocks remained in the stack?

   _____

5. Vinnie is 5 years younger than Carly. Vinnie is 15 years old. How old is Carly?

   _____

6. Mindy has $1.00. She spends $0.85 on lunch. How much money does she have left?

   _____

7. Pauline has 35 baseball cards. She buys 5 more cards. How many cards does she have altogether?

   _____

8. Matthew is 2 times as old as Greg. Greg is 6 years old. How old is Matthew?

   _____

## Mixed Review

Add, subract, multiply, or divide.

9.  $\begin{array}{r} 6 \\ \times 3 \\ \hline \end{array}$

10. $\begin{array}{r} 45 \\ +68 \\ \hline \end{array}$

11. $\begin{array}{r} 101 \\ -73 \\ \hline \end{array}$

12. $5\overline{)45}$

Fill in the missing number in the problem.

13. $\begin{array}{r} 3,672 \\ +\phantom{0000} \\ \hline 4,020 \end{array}$

14. $\begin{array}{r} 888 \\ -\phantom{000} \\ \hline 323 \end{array}$

15. $\begin{array}{r} 4 \\ \times\phantom{0} \\ \hline 36 \end{array}$

16. $9\overline{)\phantom{0}}\,^{6}$

# Collect and Organize Data

1. Make a tally table of four kinds of pets. Ask some of your classmates which pet they like best. Make a tally mark beside the name of the pet each one chooses.

2. Use the data from your tally table to make a frequency table.

3. Which type of pet did the most classmates choose? the fewest?

4. Compare your tables with those of your classmates. Did everyone get the same results?

## Mixed Review

Write >, <, or = for each ◯.

5. $6 \div 1$ ◯ $6 \div 6$

6. $10 \times 4$ ◯ $5 \times 9$

7. $12 + 12$ ◯ $10 + 13$

8. $354$ ◯ $370 - 30$

9. $236 + 3$ ◯ $239$

10. $54 \div 9$ ◯ $70 \div 10$

11. $3 \times 3$ ◯ $10 \times 1$

12. $0 \div 6$ ◯ $0 \div 7$

Solve.

13.  $\begin{array}{r} 500 \\ -\ 238 \\ \hline \end{array}$

14.  $\begin{array}{r} 104 \\ -\ 57 \\ \hline \end{array}$

15.  $\begin{array}{r} 78 \\ +\ 46 \\ \hline \end{array}$

16.  $\begin{array}{r} 518 \\ +\ 203 \\ \hline \end{array}$

17.  $\begin{array}{r} 729 \\ +\ 819 \\ \hline \end{array}$

© Harcourt

Name _____

# Understand Data

For 1–4, use the tally table.

1. List the games in order from the most to the least chosen.

   _____

   _____

   _____

| OUR FAVORITE GAMES | |
|---|---|
| Game | Tally |
| Follow-the-Leader | ⵀⵀⵀ // |
| Jump Rope | ⵀⵀⵀ ⵀⵀⵀ ⵀⵀⵀ / |
| Tether Ball | ⵀⵀⵀ ⵀⵀⵀ / |
| Four-Square | //// |

2. How many people answered the survey?

   _____

3. How many more people like jump rope than four-square?

   _____

4. How many fewer people like follow-the-leader than jump rope?

   _____

## Mixed Review

5. 106
+ 894

6. 1,219
+ 6,537

7. 9,213
− 3,219

8. 4,266
− 875

9. 8
× 4

10. 1
× 9

11. 12
× 0

12. 4
× 6

13. 7
× 7

14. Find the sum of 804 and 159. _____

15. Which number is greater: 6,232 or 6,323? _____

16. Round 2,975 to the nearest thousand. _____

© Harcourt

# Classify Data

For 1–5, use the table.

1. How many dogs have short, brown hair?

   _____

2. How many dogs have medium hair?

   _____

3. How many dogs have white hair?

   _____

| DOGS OWNED BY STUDENTS | | | | |
|---|---|---|---|---|
| | Black Hair | White Hair | Brown Hair | Golden Hair |
| Short Hair | 3 | 4 | 1 | 3 |
| Medium Hair | 2 | 2 | 0 | 1 |
| Long Hair | 1 | 3 | 3 | 2 |

4. What color hair do only 4 dogs have?

   _____

5. How many dogs are owned by the class?

   _____

6. Look at the marbles at the right. Make a table to classify, or group, the marbles.

## Mixed Review

Solve.

7. 
$$7,004$$
$$+1,664$$

8. 
$$1,241$$
$$-1,123$$

9. 
$$3,536$$
$$+5,544$$

10. 
$$9,432$$
$$-6,780$$

Name _____

# Problem Solving Strategy

## Make a Table

Solve.

1. Karen and José are doing an experiment with a spinner and a coin. They spin the pointer on the spinner and flip the coin. Then they record the results. They will repeat this experiment 15 times. Show how they could organize a table about their experiment.

2. Phillip is doing an experiment with two coins. In it, he will toss both coins 25 times and record the results after each pair of tosses. Show how he could organize a table about his experiment.

## Mixed Review

Round to the nearest 100 and 1,000.

3. 1,355 _____

4. 5,667 _____

5. 7,572 _____

6. 4,140 _____

7. 9,454 _____

8. 6,905 _____

Divide.

9. $15 \div 3 =$ _____

10. $49 \div 7 =$ _____

11. $63 \div 9 =$ _____

12. $8 \div 8 =$ _____

13. $30 \div 5 =$ _____

14. $48 \div 6 =$ _____

© Harcourt

# Problem Solving Strategy

## Make a Graph

Choose one of the ideas shown
at the right for making a pictograph.

Take a survey to collect the data.
Then make a pictograph in the
space below. Decide on a symbol
and key for the graph. Include a
title and labels.

Pictograph—Menu of Ideas
Favorite Team Sport
Favorite Pizza Topping
Favorite TV Show

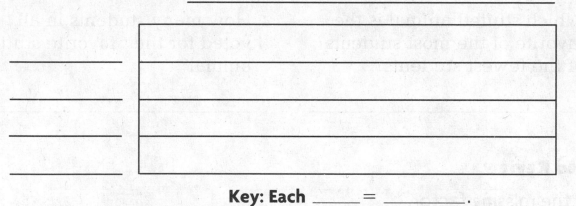

**Key: Each** _____ = _____.

1. Tell how you chose a symbol, or picture, for your pictograph.

   _____

   _____

2. Explain how you chose a key for your pictograph.

   _____

   _____

---

## Mixed Review

Write the value of the underlined digit.

3. <u>2</u>,235 _____     4. 21,<u>5</u>07 _____     5. 1<u>6</u>,110 _____

# Read Bar Graphs

For 1–4, use the bar graph.

1. What type of bar graph is this?

   _____

2. How many students named lions as their favorite stuffed animal? frogs? dogs?

   _____

   _____

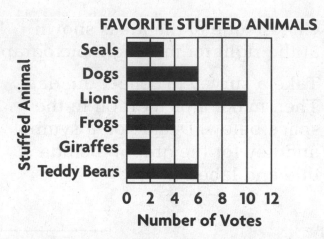

**FAVORITE STUFFED ANIMALS**

3. Which stuffed animal is the favorite of the most students? of the fewest students?

   _____

4. How many students in all voted for their favorite stuffed animal?

   _____

## Mixed Review

Find the missing factor.

5. $20 = 10 \times$ _____   6. _____ $\times 3 = 27$   7. $8 \times$ _____ $= 32$

8. _____ $\times 5 = 25$   9. $6 \times$ _____ $= 24$   10. $1 \times$ _____ $= 11$

11. $7 \times$ _____ $= 56$   12. $24 = 8 \times$ _____   13. _____ $\times 6 = 0$

Solve.

14. $12 \div 2 =$ _____   15. $7 \div 1 =$ _____   16. $8 \div 2 =$ _____

17. $9 \div 3 =$ _____   18. $10 \div 5 =$ _____   19. $6 \div 3 =$ _____

20. $9 \times 9 =$ _____   21. $6 \times 9 =$ _____   22. $4 \times 7 =$ _____

23.  6,890
    +8,054

24.  3,211
    +7,618

25.  5,765
    +5,765

26.  9,298
    +5,431

© Harcourt

## Make Bar Graphs

Make a horizontal bar graph of the data in the table at the right. Use a scale of 2. Remember to write a title and labels for the graph.

| FAVORITE DRINKS | |
|---|---|
| **Drink** | **Number of Votes** |
| Water | 4 |
| Punch | 2 |
| Milk | 5 |
| Juice | 8 |
| Soda | 12 |

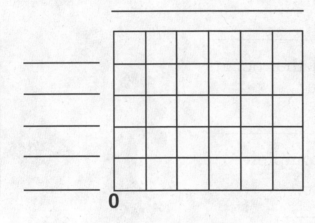

For 1–2, use your bar graph.

1. What does the graph show? _____

2. How many bars end halfway between two lines?

_____

## Mixed Review

Write $<$, $>$, or $=$ in each ◯.

3. $32 \div 8$ ◯ $1 \times 4$    4. $6 + 6$ ◯ $20$    5. $5 \times 2$ ◯ $10 - 1$

6. $7 \times 7$ ◯ $9 \times 6$    7. $18 \div 2$ ◯ $3 + 11$    8. $72 - 30$ ◯ $9 \times 3$

© Harcourt

# Line Plots

For 1–3, use the line plot at the right.

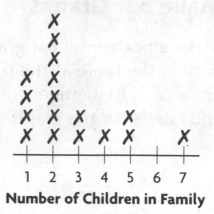

1. The **X**'s on this line plot represent the number of students. What do the numbers on the line plot represent?

   _____

2. What is the range of numbers used in this line plot?

   _____

3. What is the mode, or number that occurs most often, for this set of data?

   _____

4. Use the data in the table to complete the line plot.

| Slices of Pizza Eaten | |
| --- | --- |
| Number of Slices | Number of Students |
| 0 | // |
| 1 | ⧸⧸⧸⧸ / |
| 2 | ⧸⧸⧸⧸ |
| 3 | /// |
| 4 | / |
| 5 | // |

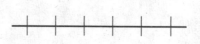

Slices of Pizza Eaten

## Mixed Review

Find each product or quotient.

5. $10 \times 7 =$ ____   6. $7 \times 9 =$ ____   7. $6 \times 1 =$ ____   8. $8 \times 2 =$ ____

9. $8 \div 4 =$ ____   10. $36 \div 6 =$ ____   11. $0 \div 22 =$ ____   12. $45 \div 9 =$ ____

© Harcourt

# Locate Points on a Grid

For 1–4, use the grid at the right. Write the letter
of the point named by the ordered pair.

**1.** (4,5) _____     **2.** (1,6) _____

**3.** (6,2) _____     **4.** (2,2) _____

For 5–10, use the grid at the right. Write the
ordered pair for each fruit.

**5.** apple _____     **6.** orange _____

**7.** banana _____     **8.** grape _____

**9.** kiwi _____     **10.** peach _____

## Mixed Review

Find the missing factor.

**11.** $3 \times$ _____ $= 21$   **12.** $4 \times$ _____ $= 16$   **13.** _____ $\times 4 = 24$

**14.** $7 \times$ _____ $= 56$   **15.** _____ $\times 9 = 54$   **16.** $5 \times$ _____ $= 50$

Solve.

**17.** $\begin{array}{r} 767 \\ -234 \\ \hline \end{array}$   **18.** $\begin{array}{r} 9,870 \\ -5,925 \\ \hline \end{array}$   **19.** $\begin{array}{r} 611 \\ +382 \\ \hline \end{array}$   **20.** $\begin{array}{r} 2,195 \\ +8,214 \\ \hline \end{array}$

**21.** $0 \times 8 =$ ___   **22.** $3 \times 5 =$ ___   **23.** $48 \div 8 =$ ___   **24.** $81 \div 9 =$ ___

**25.** $2 \times 10 =$ ___   **26.** $9 \times 8 =$ ___   **27.** $36 \div 4 =$ ___   **28.** $42 \div 7 =$ ___

**29.** $4 \times 3 =$ ___   **30.** $5 \times 6 =$ ___   **31.** $12 \div 1 =$ ___   **32.** $0 \div 7 =$ ___

# Read Line Graphs

For 1–4, use the line graph at the right.

1. Joyce made this line graph to show the number of pages she read each day in a mystery book. On what day did Joyce read the most pages? the fewest?

_____

2. How many pages did Joyce read on Thursday?

_____

3. On which two days did Joyce read the same number of pages?

_____

4. How many more pages did Joyce read on Friday than on Monday?

_____

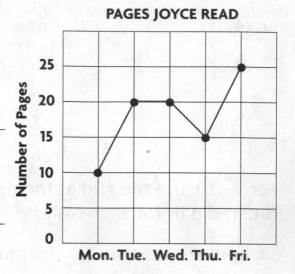

**PAGES JOYCE READ**

# Mixed Review

Solve.

5. 3)18

6. 5)25

7. 6)24

8. 7)63

9. 10)10

10. 8)24

11. 10)20

12. 2)14

13.   1,234
    +5,673

14.   3,179
    +3,298

15.   2,051
    −1,009

16.   8,233
    −4,649

# Certain and Impossible

## Vocabulary

Fill in the blank with the correct word.

event                    certain                    impossible

1. An event is _____ if it will never happen.

2. An _____ is something that happens.

3. An event is _____ if it will always happen.

_____

Tell whether each event is *certain* or *impossible*.

4. Pencils will fall from the sky.

_____

5. Winter in Alaska is cold.

_____

6. You will walk to the moon tonight.

_____

7. Putting your hand in boiling water will burn you.

_____

For 8–9, use the numbered tile. Tell whether each event is *certain* or *impossible*.

| 1 | 3 | 3 |
| 1 | 5 | 7 |
| 3 | 5 | 7 |

8. dropping a coin on an odd number _____

9. dropping a coin on a number greater than 9 _____

## Mixed Review

Find the sum or the difference.

| 10. | 11. | 12. | 13. | 14. |
|---|---|---|---|---|
| 75<br>+39 | 94<br>+28 | 19<br>+26 | 47<br>−38 | 66<br>−27 |

| 15. | 16. | 17. | 18. |
|---|---|---|---|
| 86<br>−36 | 943<br>−218 | 208<br>−109 | 705<br>−329 |

Find the product.

19. $9 \times 8 =$ ___    20. $7 \times 6 =$ ___    21. $6 \times 4 =$ ___    22. $5 \times 9 =$ ___

# Likely and Unlikely

For 1–2, tell whether each event is *likely* or *unlikely*.

1. having the same birthday as 5 other classmates _____

2. eating a piece of fruit—or some food with fruit in it—today _____

For 3–4, look at the set of cards and spinner.

3. Suppose these cards are mixed up and placed face-down. If you turn over one card, which number are you unlikely to choose? Why?

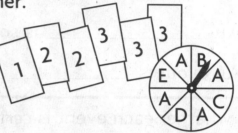

_____

_____

4. Which letter on the spinner are you likely to spin? Explain.

_____

_____

## Mixed Review

5. $9\overline{)81}$    6. $5\overline{)10}$    7. $6\overline{)36}$    8. $7\overline{)49}$

9. $4\overline{)40}$    10. $3\overline{)24}$    11. $7\overline{)56}$    12. $10\overline{)20}$

13. $\begin{array}{r} 9 \\ \times 3 \\ \hline \end{array}$    14. $\begin{array}{r} 7 \\ \times 6 \\ \hline \end{array}$    15. $\begin{array}{r} 4 \\ \times 8 \\ \hline \end{array}$    16. $\begin{array}{r} 6 \\ \times 6 \\ \hline \end{array}$

17. $\begin{array}{r} 9 \\ \times 2 \\ \hline \end{array}$    18. $\begin{array}{r} 5 \\ \times 7 \\ \hline \end{array}$    19. $\begin{array}{r} 9 \\ \times 5 \\ \hline \end{array}$    20. $\begin{array}{r} 3 \\ \times 7 \\ \hline \end{array}$

© Harcourt

# Possible Outcomes

For 1–4, list the possible outcomes of each event.

1. dropping a marker on one of these squares

| 1 | | |
|---|---|---|
| 3 | 11 | |
| 5 | 7 | 9 |

_____

2. pulling a number from this bag

_____

3. rolling a cube labeled A–F

_____

4. using this spinner

_____

5. Karen has a bag of 4 blue balls, 2 green balls, and 1 red ball. What is the chance that she will pull a green ball from the bag?

_____

6. Martin spins the pointer. What is his chance of spinning a square?

_____

7. Gia used this spinner. The pointer landed on black 1 time, and on white 1 time. Predict the color it will land on next. What is the chance she will spin gray?

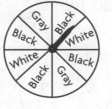

_____

## Mixed Review

Write the fraction that names the white part of the spinner.

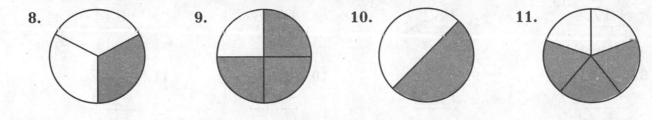

8. _____  9. _____  10. _____  11. _____

# Experiments

Read the following experiment.

Marsha has a bag filled with 20 tiles. There are 7 blue, 2 green, 4 yellow, and 7 red tiles. She pulls a tile from the bag 10 times. Below is a list of the outcomes of the 10 pulls.

| | |
|---|---|
| 1–red | 6–red |
| 2–blue | 7–blue |
| 3–red | 8–yellow |
| 4–yellow | 9–red |
| 5–green | 10–blue |

Record the results in the tally table.

Use your tally table to answer 1–3.

| MARSHA'S EXPERIMENT | |
|---|---|
| Color | Tally |
| Red | |
| Blue | |
| Yellow | |
| Green | |

1. What color did she pull most often?

   _____

2. What color did she pull least often?

   _____

3. Why do you think this is so?

   _____

   _____

## Mixed Review

Solve.

4.    33
    +17
   _____

5.    79
    +82
   _____

6.    543
    +108
   _____

7.    412
    +344
   _____

8.    190
    +150
   _____

9.    222
    +279
   _____

10.   987
    +213
   _____

11.   557
    +904
   _____

12. $10 \times 4 =$ _____

13. _____ $\times 9 = 27$

14. $5 \times$ _____ $= 40$

Name _____

# Predict Outcomes

1. This tally table shows the pulls from a bag of tiles. Predict which color is most likely to be pulled.

| Tally Table | |
|---|---|
| **Color** | **Tallies** |
| black | ⅢⅢ |
| green | Ⅲ |
| red | ⅢⅢ ⅢⅢ Ⅱ |

_____

2. The line plot below shows the results of rolling a number cube. Predict which number you would most likely roll.

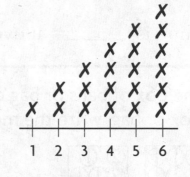

_____

3. This tally table shows the results of using a spinner. Predict whether the spinner will land on blue or red on the next spin.

| Tally Table | |
|---|---|
| **Color** | **Tallies** |
| blue | ⅢⅢ ⅢⅢ ⅢⅢ Ⅰ |
| red | ⅢⅢ ⅢⅢ ⅢⅢ Ⅰ |

_____

4. This tally table shows the pulls from a bag of balls. Predict which color is least likely to be pulled.

| Tally Table | |
|---|---|
| **Color** | **Tallies** |
| blue | ⅢⅢ ⅢⅢ ⅢⅢ ⅢⅢ |
| white | Ⅱ |
| purple | ⅢⅢ ⅢⅢ Ⅲ |

_____

## Mixed Review

Complete.

5. 35¢ = _____ pennies

6. $2.00 = _____ dimes

7. 75¢ = _____ quarters

8. 65¢ = _____ nickels

Underline the number that is less.

9. 35 or 54

10. 91 or 88

11. 110 or 100

Name _____

# Problem Solving Skill

## Draw Conclusions

### Vocabulary

Fill in the blank.

1. A game is _____ if every player has an equal chance to win.

---

Circle the box of balls or bag of letters that is fair. For each unfair box or bag, write the most likely outcome.

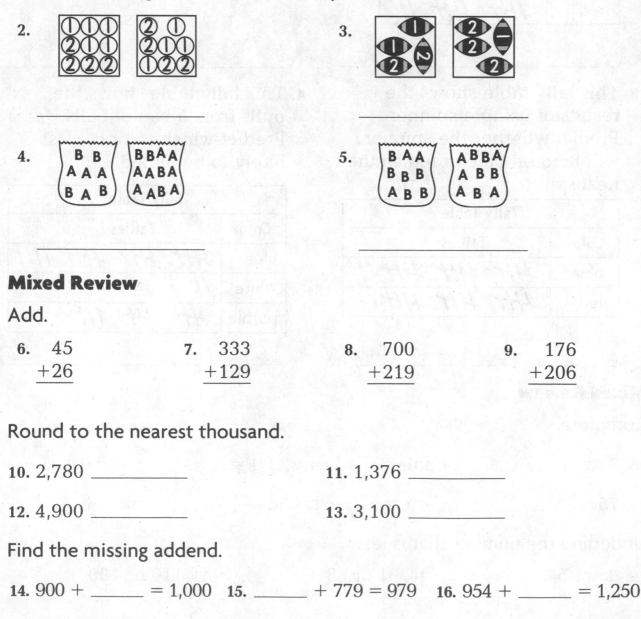

2. _____

3. _____

4. _____

5. _____

## Mixed Review

Add.

6.  45
   +26

7.  333
   +129

8.  700
   +219

9.  176
   +206

Round to the nearest thousand.

10. 2,780 _____

11. 1,376 _____

12. 4,900 _____

13. 3,100 _____

Find the missing addend.

14. 900 + _____ = 1,000  15. _____ + 779 = 979  16. 954 + _____ = 1,250

# Multiply 2-Digit Numbers

Use the array to help find the product.

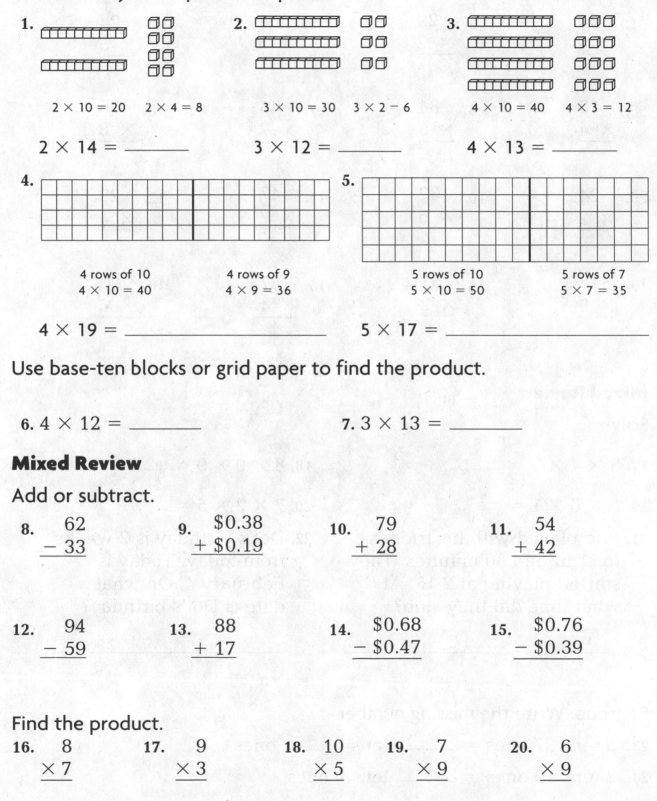

1. $2 \times 10 = 20$   $2 \times 4 = 8$

$2 \times 14 = $ _____

2. $3 \times 10 = 30$   $3 \times 2 = 6$

$3 \times 12 = $ _____

3. $4 \times 10 = 40$   $4 \times 3 = 12$

$4 \times 13 = $ _____

4.

| 4 rows of 10 | 4 rows of 9 |
|---|---|
| $4 \times 10 = 40$ | $4 \times 9 = 36$ |

$4 \times 19 = $ _____

5.

| 5 rows of 10 | 5 rows of 7 |
|---|---|
| $5 \times 10 = 50$ | $5 \times 7 = 35$ |

$5 \times 17 = $ _____

Use base-ten blocks or grid paper to find the product.

6. $4 \times 12 = $ _____

7. $3 \times 13 = $ _____

## Mixed Review

Add or subtract.

8.
$$\begin{array}{r} 62 \\ -33 \\ \hline \end{array}$$

9.
$$\begin{array}{r} \$0.38 \\ +\$0.19 \\ \hline \end{array}$$

10.
$$\begin{array}{r} 79 \\ +28 \\ \hline \end{array}$$

11.
$$\begin{array}{r} 54 \\ +42 \\ \hline \end{array}$$

12.
$$\begin{array}{r} 94 \\ -59 \\ \hline \end{array}$$

13.
$$\begin{array}{r} 88 \\ +17 \\ \hline \end{array}$$

14.
$$\begin{array}{r} \$0.68 \\ -\$0.47 \\ \hline \end{array}$$

15.
$$\begin{array}{r} \$0.76 \\ -\$0.39 \\ \hline \end{array}$$

Find the product.

16.
$$\begin{array}{r} 8 \\ \times 7 \\ \hline \end{array}$$

17.
$$\begin{array}{r} 9 \\ \times 3 \\ \hline \end{array}$$

18.
$$\begin{array}{r} 10 \\ \times 5 \\ \hline \end{array}$$

19.
$$\begin{array}{r} 7 \\ \times 9 \\ \hline \end{array}$$

20.
$$\begin{array}{r} 6 \\ \times 9 \\ \hline \end{array}$$

# Record Multiplication

Find the product. You may wish to use base-ten blocks.

1.  $56 \times 4$

2.  $29 \times 2$

3.  $64 \times 3$

4.  $24 \times 5$

5.  $13 \times 4$

6.  $84 \times 5$

7.  $45 \times 7$

8.  $36 \times 8$

9.  $24 \times 2$

10. $32 \times 6$

11. $47 \times 7$

12. $29 \times 4$

13. $18 \times 3$

14. $51 \times 2$

15. $27 \times 4$

16. $33 \times 6$

## Mixed Review

Solve.

17. $3 \times 4 \times 2 =$ _____

18. $8 \times 0 \times 9 =$ _____

19. $5 \times 6 \times 1 =$ _____

20. $7 \times 2 \times 5 =$ _____

21. Bob played with his friends for 1 hr and 30 minutes. They started playing at 2:15. At what time did they stop?

22. Dot's birthday is 2 weeks from today. Today is February 4. On what date is Dot's birthday?

_____

_____

Regroup. Write the missing number.

23. 5 tens 27 ones = _____ tens _____ ones

24. 2 tens 19 ones = _____ tens 9 ones

25. _____ tens 31 ones = 8 tens 1 one

Name _____

# Practice Multiplication

Find the product. Tell whether you need to regroup.
Write *yes* or *no*.

1. 96 × 3

2. 21 × 2

3. 83 × 5

4. 56 × 6

5. 71 × 3

6. 45 × 2

7. 69 × 5

8. 83 × 3

Find the product.

9. 75 × 3

10. 28 × 7

11. 16 × 4

12. 33 × 2

13. $2 \times 84 =$

14. $3 \times 64 =$

15. $5 \times 32 =$

## Mixed Review

Write the value of the underlined digit.

16. 86,459 _____

17. 342,196 _____

18. 74,598 _____

19. 2,437 _____

20. 69,438 _____

21. 11,302 _____

Complete.

22. ___ $\times 9 = 36$

23. $56 =$ ___ $\times 8$

24. $6 \times$ ___ $= 54$

25. $17 +$ ___ $= 44$

26. ___ $- 9 = 43$

27. $21 +$ ___ $= 64$

28. ___ $\times 8 = 56$

29. $7 \times$ ___ $= 28$

30. $5 \times$ ___ $= 45$

31. $59 -$ ___ $= 31$

32. $22 +$ ___ $= 30$

33. $38 +$ ___ $= 55$

34. $9 \times$ ___ $= 36$

35. ___ $\times 5 = 40$

36. $7 \times$ ___ $= 49$

Name _____

# Problem Solving Skill

## Choose the Operation

Write whether you would *add*, *subtract*, *multiply*, or *divide*. Then solve.

1. Susan's family paid $36 for 4 used videos. Each video cost the same amount. How much did each video cost?

_____

2. A third-grade class learns 18 spelling words one week and 16 the next week. How many words does the class learn in 2 weeks?

_____

3. A lunch room seats 84 students. If there are 56 students in the lunch room, how many more students can the lunch room hold?

_____

4. Maria has written 24 pages in her diary. She puts 3 daily entries on each page. How many daily entries has she written?

_____

## Mixed Review

Find the sum.

| 5. | 6. | 7. | 8. | 9. | 10. |
|---|---|---|---|---|---|
| 14 | 29 | 63 | 47 | 20 | 83 |
| 15 | 8 | 30 | 114 | 67 | 25 |
| + 18 | + 77 | + 49 | + 142 | + 38 | + 71 |

| 11. | 12. | 13. | 14. | 15. |
|---|---|---|---|---|
| 753 | 934 | 295 | 854 | 717 |
| + 495 | + 248 | + 692 | + 196 | + 362 |

| 16. | 17. | 18. | 19. | 20. |
|---|---|---|---|---|
| 4,762 | 9,132 | 5,689 | 1,911 | 7,571 |
| + 3,291 | + 4,376 | + 8,542 | + 8,149 | + 6,025 |

| 21. | 22. | 23. | 24. | 25. |
|---|---|---|---|---|
| $14.29 | $ 4.10 | $2.05 | $62.77 | $41.95 |
| + $ 6.33 | + $27.19 | + $8.99 | + $18.19 | + $27.42 |

© Harcourt

# Mental Math: Patterns in Multiplication

Complete. Use patterns and mental math to help.

1. $9 \times 1 =$ _____
   $9 \times 10 =$ _____
   $9 \times 100 =$ _____
   $9 \times 1,000 =$ _____

2. $6 \times 3 =$ _____
   $6 \times 30 =$ _____
   $6 \times 300 =$ _____
   $6 \times 3,000 =$ _____

3. $7 \times 4 =$ _____
   _____ $\times 40 = 280$
   $7 \times$ _____ $= 2,800$
   $7 \times 4,000 =$ _____

4. $6 \times 5 =$ _____
   _____ $\times 50 = 300$
   $6 \times$ _____ $= 3,000$
   $6 \times 5,000 =$ _____

Use mental math and basic facts to complete.

5. $7 \times 80 =$ _____
6. $9 \times$ _____ $= 45,000$
7. _____ $\times 60 = 240$

8. $2 \times$ _____ $= 1,400$
9. $7 \times$ _____ $= 42,000$
10. _____ $\times 800 = 2,400$

11. _____ $\times 20 = 180$
12. $5 \times 500 =$ _____
13. $5 \times 4,000 =$ _____

14. $3 \times$ _____ $= 210$
15. $1 \times$ _____ $= 1,000$
16. $5 \times 200 =$ _____

## Mixed Review

Find the product or quotient.

17. $\begin{array}{r} 35 \\ \times 7 \\ \hline \end{array}$
18. $\begin{array}{r} 62 \\ \times 7 \\ \hline \end{array}$
19. $\begin{array}{r} 58 \\ \times 3 \\ \hline \end{array}$
20. $\begin{array}{r} 47 \\ \times 5 \\ \hline \end{array}$
21. $\begin{array}{r} 24 \\ \times 6 \\ \hline \end{array}$

22. $36 \div 6 =$ _____
23. $18 \div 6 =$ _____
24. $10 \times 6 =$ _____

25. $81 \div 9 =$ _____
26. $7 \times 6 =$ _____
27. $56 \div 8 =$ _____

# Problem Solving Strategy

## Find a Pattern

Find a pattern to solve.

1. A dictionary contains the definitions of 3,000 words. How many words do 5 dictionaries contain?

_____

2. One box can hold 400 file folders. How many file folders can 9 boxes hold?

_____

3. One sheet of grid paper has 900 squares on it. How many squares do 8 sheets of grid paper have altogether?

_____

4. A tourist bus travels 400 miles each day. How many miles will the bus travel in 4 days?

_____

5. For fun, Betty jumps rope 200 times each day. How many jumps will she do in 5 days?

_____

6. Kevin rides his bike 60 miles each month. How many miles does he ride his bike in 6 months?

_____

7. Colleen bought a purse decorated with 800 shiny beads. How many beads would 3 purses have altogether?

_____

8. Neil spent $900 on a new refrigerator. How much would 6 new refrigerators cost?

_____

## Mixed Review

Divide and check.

9. $3\overline{)27}$    10. $5\overline{)45}$    11. $6\overline{)48}$    12. $4\overline{)32}$    13. $8\overline{)16}$

Multiply.

14. $\begin{array}{r} 67 \\ \times\ 6 \\ \hline \end{array}$    15. $\begin{array}{r} 83 \\ \times\ 9 \\ \hline \end{array}$    16. $\begin{array}{r} 52 \\ \times\ 7 \\ \hline \end{array}$    17. $\begin{array}{r} 29 \\ \times\ 5 \\ \hline \end{array}$    18. $\begin{array}{r} 46 \\ \times\ 3 \\ \hline \end{array}$

# Estimate Products

Estimate the product.

1. 52
$\times 7$

2. 47
$\times 6$

3. 26
$\times 4$

4. 92
$\times 8$

5. 98
$\times 3$

6. 75
$\times 2$

7. 316
$\times 3$

8. 451
$\times 7$

9. 845
$\times 5$

10. 942
$\times 3$

11. 651
$\times 8$

12. 327
$\times 4$

13. 29
$\times 8$

14. 32
$\times 6$

15. 759
$\times 9$

16. 452
$\times 6$

17. 649
$\times 3$

18. 82
$\times 2$

19. 256
$\times 4$

20. 719
$\times 5$

## Mixed Review

Add or subtract.

21. 834
$-509$

22. 951
$-843$

23. 917
$-603$

24. 508
$+293$

25. 672
$+109$

26. $5.68
$- \$2.19$

27. $7.34
$- \$0.88$

28. $4.00
$- \$0.09$

29. $2.98
$+ \$6.09$

30. $9.05
$+ \$3.94$

Multiply.

31. 33
$\times 7$

32. 49
$\times 3$

33. 61
$\times 8$

34. 82
$\times 5$

35. 17
$\times 9$

Name _____

# Multiply 3-Digit Numbers

Multiply. Tell each place you need to regroup.

| 1. 354<br>× 5 | 2. 726<br>× 3 | 3. 119<br>× 7 | 4. 329<br>× 2 | 5. 153<br>× 4 |
|---|---|---|---|---|

Find the product. Estimate to check.

| 6. 576<br>× 9 | 7. 925<br>× 7 | 8. 163<br>× 2 | 9. 238<br>× 3 | 10. 412<br>× 5 |
|---|---|---|---|---|

Find the product.

| 11. 248<br>× 6 | 12. 713<br>× 7 | 13. 637<br>× 9 | 14. 362<br>× 8 | 15. 425<br>× 7 |
|---|---|---|---|---|
| 16. 462<br>× 5 | 17. 183<br>× 8 | 18. 279<br>× 6 | 19. 493<br>× 5 | 20. 356<br>× 7 |
| 21. 358<br>× 4 | 22. 920<br>× 6 | 23. 872<br>× 3 | 24. 516<br>× 4 | 25. 432<br>× 5 |

## Mixed Review

Write the time.

26.

27.

28.

Name _____

# Find Products Using Money

Find the product in dollars and cents. Estimate to check.

| 1. $7.54<br>× 4 | 2. $6.26<br>× 7 | 3. $8.19<br>× 6 | 4. $5.24<br>× 5 | 5. $3.61<br>× 3 |
|---|---|---|---|---|
| 6. $3.76<br>× 8 | 7. $4.25<br>× 9 | 8. $2.63<br>× 3 | 9. $5.90<br>× 4 | 10. $3.24<br>× 7 |

Find the product in dollars and cents.

| 11. $9.48<br>× 2 | 12. $7.13<br>× 5 | 13. $8.37<br>× 9 | 14. $2.36<br>× 6 | 15. $1.25<br>× 9 |
|---|---|---|---|---|
| 16. $2.62<br>× 4 | 17. $7.83<br>× 6 | 18. $9.79<br>× 2 | 19. $4.91<br>× 3 | 20. $6.82<br>× 4 |
| 21. $8.58<br>× 3 | 22. $6.20<br>× 7 | 23. $5.72<br>× 8 | 24. $5.45<br>× 2 | 25. $2.15<br>× 5 |

## Mixed Review

Write vertically. Add or subtract.

26. $14.52 − $2.13 = _____      27. $14.52 + $2.13 = _____

28. $17.28 + $12.99 = _____      29. $17.28 − $12.99 = _____

# Practice Multiplication

Find the product. Estimate to check.

1. 6,754
   × 3

2. $36.56
   × 5

3. 3,919
   × 7

4. 4,214
   × 3

5. 6,521
   × 5

6. $53.76
   × 4

7. 6,425
   × 8

8. 3,863
   × 2

9. 7,338
   × 2

10. 2,462
    × 4

Find the product.

11. $59.48
    × 3

12. 5,413
    × 6

13. 7,237
    × 5

14. 2,134
    × 8

15. $7.68
    × 2

16. 9,262
    × 7

17. $70.83
    × 4

18. 179
    × 9

19. 564
    × 6

20. 4,312
    × 5

21. 1,958
    × 2

22. 6,020
    × 8

23. 978
    × 8

24. 1,236
    × 7

25. 512
    × 9

26. $5 \times 2,317 =$ _____

27. _____ $= 6 \times 5,912$

## Mixed Review

Complete.

28. $4 \times 7 =$ _____

$4 \times 70 =$ _____

$4 \times 700 =$ _____

$4 \times 7,000 =$ _____

29. $6 \times 9 =$ _____

$6 \times 90 =$ _____

$6 \times 900 =$ _____

$6 \times 9,000 =$ _____

# Divide with Remainders

## Vocabulary

Fill in the blank.

1. In division, the _____ is the amount left over when a number cannot be divided evenly.

---

Use counters to find the quotient and remainder.

2. $13 \div 3 =$ _____

3. $15 \div 2 =$ _____

4. $11 \div 4 =$ _____

5. $12 \div 5 =$ _____

6. $10 \div 4 =$ _____

7. $9 \div 5 =$ _____

Find the quotient and remainder. You may use counters or draw a picture to help.

8. $17 \div 3 =$ _____

9. $13 \div 4 =$ _____

10. $23 \div 4 =$ _____

11. $30 \div 4 =$ _____

12. $25 \div 3 =$ _____

13. $17 \div 4 =$ _____

## Mixed Review

Find the difference. Estimate to check.

14. $432 - 251 =$

15. $847 - 563 =$

16. $712 - 386 =$

_____

_____

_____

17. $598 - 202 -$

18. $\$6.29 - \$3.84 =$

19. $515 - 409 =$

_____

_____

_____

20. $\$7.06 - \$4.37 =$

21. $824 - 399 =$

22. $918 - 264 =$

_____

_____

_____

© Harcourt

# Model Division of 2-Digit Numbers

Use the model. Write the quotient and remainder.

1. $51 \div 2 =$ ?

_____.

2. $38 \div 3 =$ ?

_____.

Divide. You may use base-ten blocks to help.

3. $2\overline{)53}$      4. $4\overline{)61}$      5. $2\overline{)17}$

6. $5\overline{)63}$      7. $5\overline{)48}$      8. $3\overline{)48}$

## Mixed Review

Find the difference.

9.  $\begin{array}{r} 7,658 \\ -1,947 \end{array}$   10.  $\begin{array}{r} 8,000 \\ -2,503 \end{array}$   11.  $\begin{array}{r} 5,468 \\ -3,846 \end{array}$   12.  $\begin{array}{r} \$39.59 \\ -\$17.64 \end{array}$   13.  $\begin{array}{r} 9,046 \\ -4,108 \end{array}$

14.  $\begin{array}{r} 3,417 \\ -1,908 \end{array}$   15.  $\begin{array}{r} 1,754 \\ -\phantom{0}862 \end{array}$   16.  $\begin{array}{r} 21,086 \\ -17,497 \end{array}$   17.  $\begin{array}{r} 4,325 \\ -\phantom{0}648 \end{array}$   18.  $\begin{array}{r} 6,023 \\ -5,100 \end{array}$

# Record Division of 2-Digit Numbers

Divide and check.

1. $72 \div 7 =$ _____

2. $49 \div 6 =$ _____

3. $88 \div 8 =$ _____

4. $6\overline{)34}$

5. $7\overline{)19}$

6. $5\overline{)59}$

Write the check step for each division problem.

| | Check: | | Check: | | Check: |
|---|---|---|---|---|---|
| 7. $5\overline{)27}$ | | 8. $3\overline{)48}$ | | 9. $4\overline{)65}$ | |

## Mixed Review

Find the product.

10. $\begin{array}{r} 13 \\ \times\ 6 \\ \hline \end{array}$

11. $\begin{array}{r} 21 \\ \times\ 3 \\ \hline \end{array}$

12. $\begin{array}{r} 53 \\ \times\ 5 \\ \hline \end{array}$

13. $\begin{array}{r} 36 \\ \times\ 4 \\ \hline \end{array}$

14. $\begin{array}{r} 19 \\ \times\ 1 \\ \hline \end{array}$

15. $\begin{array}{r} 48 \\ \times\ 7 \\ \hline \end{array}$

16. $\begin{array}{r} 16 \\ \times\ 5 \\ \hline \end{array}$

17. $\begin{array}{r} 43 \\ \times\ 7 \\ \hline \end{array}$

18. $\begin{array}{r} 38 \\ \times\ 3 \\ \hline \end{array}$

19. $\begin{array}{r} 29 \\ \times\ 6 \\ \hline \end{array}$

20. $\begin{array}{r} 50 \\ \times\ 4 \\ \hline \end{array}$

21. $\begin{array}{r} 17 \\ \times\ 8 \\ \hline \end{array}$

# Practice Division

Divide and check.

1. 29 ÷ 4 = _____     2. 67 ÷ 5 = _____     3. 63 ÷ 4 = _____

Check:                    Check:                    Check:

4. 56 ÷ 3 = _____     5. 39 ÷ 2 = _____     6. 51 ÷ 3 = _____

Check:                    Check:                    Check:

## Mixed Review

Write the missing factor.

7. 24 = 8 × ■        8. 45 = ■ × 5        9. 9 × ■ = 81        10. 100 = 10 × ■

_____        _____        _____        _____

11. 12 = 4 × ■        12. 18 = 2 × ■        13. 7 × ■ = 63        14. 64 = 8 × ■

_____        _____        _____        _____

Name _____

# Problem Solving Skill
## Interpret the Remainder

1. Alexandra has 74 baseball cards in a collection. She can fit 9 cards on a page. How many pages does she need?

_____

2. Roger is making kites. It takes 6 feet of string to make a kite. He has 80 feet of string. How many kites can he make?

_____

3. Clem has 63 books. He wants to put an equal number of books on each of 5 shelves. The rest of the books he will donate to a library. How many books will Clem donate to a library?

_____

4. George is making toast. His toaster toasts 2 slices of bread at one time. He cannot toast one slice at a time in his toaster. He has 19 pieces of bread. How many times will he use his toaster?

_____

5. Rob has 32 snacks that he needs to pack equally into 5 boxes. How many snacks will be in each box?

_____

6. Mary and 12 of her friends are going on a bus trip. Each seat on the bus holds three. How many seats will they need?

_____

## Mixed Review

Divide and check.

7. $9\overline{)37}$

8. $8\overline{)46}$

9. $4\overline{)58}$

Subtract.

10.  $\begin{array}{r} 4,236 \\ -3,572 \\ \hline \end{array}$

11.  $\begin{array}{r} 3,502 \\ -2,508 \\ \hline \end{array}$

12.  $\begin{array}{r} 4,003 \\ -3,927 \\ \hline \end{array}$

13.  $\begin{array}{r} 8,611 \\ -7,844 \\ \hline \end{array}$

© Harcourt

# Mental Math: Patterns in Division

Complete. Use patterns and mental math.

1. $36 \div 4 =$ _____

$360 \div 4 =$ _____

$3,600 \div 4 =$ _____

2. $54 \div 6 =$ _____

$540 \div 6 =$ _____

$5,400 \div 6 =$ _____

3. $25 \div 5 =$ _____

_____ $\div 5 = 50$

$2,500 \div 5 =$ _____

4. $27 \div 9 =$ _____

_____ $\div 9 = 30$

$2,700 \div$ _____ $= 300$

5. $18 \div 2 =$ _____

_____ $\div 2 = 90$

$1,800 \div$ _____ $= 900$

6. $49 \div 7 =$ _____

$490 \div 7 =$ _____

_____ $\div 7 = 700$

Use mental math and a basic fact to find the quotient.

7. $2,000 \div 5 =$ _____

8. $5,600 \div 7 =$ _____

9. $3,000 \div 6 =$ _____

10. $900 \div 3 =$ _____

11. $1,500 \div 5 =$ _____

12. $2,800 \div 4 =$ _____

13. $450 \div 9 =$ _____

14. $6,300 \div 7 =$ _____

15. $640 \div 8 =$ _____

16. $400 \div 5 =$ _____

17. $3,500 \div 7 =$ _____

18. $200 \div 2 =$ _____

19. $1,600 \div 4 =$ _____

20. $6,000 \div 2 =$ _____

21. $250 \div 5 =$ _____

## Mixed Review

Find the quotient.

22. $8\overline{)36}$

23. $9\overline{)46}$

24. $8\overline{)76}$

25. $7\overline{)43}$

Find the product.

26. $8 \times 6 =$ _____

27. $7 \times 9 =$ _____

28. $4 \times 7 =$ _____

29. $6 \times 6 =$ _____

30. $10 \times 5 =$ _____

31. $8 \times 3 =$ _____

32. $5 \times 7 =$ _____

33. $9 \times 8 =$ _____

34. $7 \times 8 =$ _____

© Harcourt

# Estimate Quotients

Estimate each quotient. Write the basic fact you used to find the estimate.

**1.** $179 \div 3$

**2.** $484 \div 7$

**3.** $199 \div 4$

_____

_____

_____

**4.** $416 \div 6$

**5.** $648 \div 9$

**6.** $137 \div 2$

_____

_____

_____

Estimate the quotient.

**7.** $148 \div 5 =$ _____

**8.** $134 \div 7 =$ _____

**9.** $268 \div 3 =$ _____

**10.** $555 \div 7 =$ _____

**11.** $538 \div 9 =$ _____

**12.** $334 \div 8 =$ _____

**13.** $3\overline{)142}$

**14.** $7\overline{)500}$

**15.** $3\overline{)299}$

**16.** $5\overline{)444}$

**17.** $8\overline{)317}$

**18.** $8\overline{)635}$

## Mixed Review

Divide and check.

**19.** $9\overline{)36}$

**20.** $7\overline{)49}$

**21.** $3\overline{)15}$

**22.** $5\overline{)45}$

**23.** $9\overline{)81}$

**24.** $6\overline{)54}$

**25.** $9\overline{)54}$

**26.** $4\overline{)32}$

Multiply.

**17.** $\begin{array}{r} 438 \\ \times\ 6 \\ \hline \end{array}$

**18.** $\begin{array}{r} 517 \\ \times\ 4 \\ \hline \end{array}$

**19.** $\begin{array}{r} 629 \\ \times\ 3 \\ \hline \end{array}$

**20.** $\begin{array}{r} 804 \\ \times\ 7 \\ \hline \end{array}$

# Place the First Digit in the Quotient

Place an X where the first digit in the quotient should be.

1. $5\overline{)252}$

2. $3\overline{)156}$

3. $6\overline{)96}$

4. $7\overline{)497}$

Find the quotient.

5. $3\overline{)123}$

6. $6\overline{)204}$

7. $9\overline{)324}$

8. $3\overline{)279}$

9. $4\overline{)88}$

10. $7\overline{)329}$

11. $4\overline{)352}$

12. $6\overline{)384}$

13. $5\overline{)310}$

14. $8\overline{)408}$

15. $2\overline{)112}$

16. $4\overline{)180}$

## Mixed Review

Multiply.

17. $\begin{array}{r} 435 \\ \times\ 6 \\ \hline \end{array}$

18. $\begin{array}{r} 176 \\ \times\ 6 \\ \hline \end{array}$

19. $\begin{array}{r} 826 \\ \times\ 6 \\ \hline \end{array}$

20. $\begin{array}{r} 532 \\ \times\ 6 \\ \hline \end{array}$

21. $\begin{array}{r} 154 \\ \times\ 5 \\ \hline \end{array}$

22. $\begin{array}{r} 278 \\ \times\ 7 \\ \hline \end{array}$

23. $\begin{array}{r} 814 \\ \times\ 2 \\ \hline \end{array}$

24. $\begin{array}{r} 302 \\ \times\ 8 \\ \hline \end{array}$

What time does each clock show?

25. _____

26. _____

27. _____

# Practice Division of 3-Digit Numbers

Find the quotient.

1. 5)810
2. 3)963
3. 6)948
4. 7)952

5. 4)392
6. 2)830
7. 7)924
8. 5)255

9. 2)174
10. 9)675
11. 8)744
12. 3)762

## Mixed Review

Multiply.

13. 2,421
    ×   3

14. 3,176
    ×   8

15. 1,826
    ×   7

16. 3,521
    ×   4

17. 9,438
    ×   5

18. 2,425
    ×   2

19. 4,434
    ×   6

20. 1,052
    ×   9

© Harcourt

Name _____

# Divide Amounts of Money

Find the quotient.

1. 4)$9.08     2. 3)$8.19     3. 4)$6.12     4. 5)$6.50

5. 2)$7.12     6. 6)$9.54     7. 7)$7.98     8. 6)$6.78

9. 5)$9.80     10. 9)$6.57    11. 8)$9.28    12. 4)$8.68

## Mixed Review

Find the sum or difference.

13.  381      14.  892      15.  520      16.  176
    +746          − 467         − 363         + 859

17.  $2.04    18.  $9.00    19.  $3.16    20.  $7.59
    + $8.78       − $6.35       + $4.87       − $1.96

Add.

21. 82 + 147 + 63 + 298 = _____    22. 119 + 43 + 158 + 76 = _____

# Problem Solving Strategy

## Solve a Simpler Problem

For 1–4, *solve a simpler problem*.

**1.** There are 800 children that need to be put into 5 groups. How many students should be in each group?

_____

_____

_____

_____

**2.** There are 325 children that need to be put into 5 groups. How many students should be in each group?

_____

_____

_____

_____

**3.** Larry has $7.00 in nickels. How many nickels does he have?

_____

_____

_____

_____

**4.** Terry has $80.00 in dimes. How many dimes does she have?

_____

_____

_____

_____

## Mixed Review

Divide.

**5.** $2\overline{)\$3.50}$    **6.** $5\overline{)\$5.75}$    **7.** $4\overline{)\$7.64}$    **8.** $6\overline{)\$8.70}$

Multiply.

**9.**  $\begin{array}{r} 82 \\ \times\ 7 \\ \hline \end{array}$    **10.**  $\begin{array}{r} 192 \\ \times\ 5 \\ \hline \end{array}$    **11.**  $\begin{array}{r} 2,683 \\ \times\ \ \ 4 \\ \hline \end{array}$    **12.**  $\begin{array}{r} 1,365 \\ \times\ \ \ 8 \\ \hline \end{array}$

# Solid Figures

Name the solid figure that each object looks like.

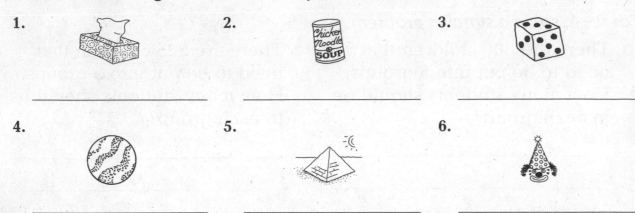

1. _____

2. _____

3. _____

4. _____

5. _____

6. _____

Complete the table.

| | Figure | Faces | Edges | Vertices |
|---|---|---|---|---|
| 7. | Cube | | | |
| 8. | Rectangular Prism | | | |
| 9. | Square Pyramid | | | |
| 10. | Sphere | | | |

## Mixed Review

Circle the number that is greater.

11. 3,535      12. 67,100      13. 53,606      14. 9,999

    3,355          67,099        53,701       10,000

Find the quotient.

15. $25 \div 5 =$ ___ 16. $45 \div 9 =$ ___ 17. $35 \div 7 =$ ___ 18. $50 \div 10 =$ ___

19. $49 \div 7 =$ ___ 20. $15 \div 5 =$ ___ 21. $81 \div 9 =$ ___ 22. $54 \div 6 =$ ___

Find the difference.

23. $25 - 5 =$ ___ 24. $45 - 9 =$ ___ 25. $35 - 7 =$ ___ 26. $50 - 10 =$ ___

27. $49 - 7 =$ ___ 28. $15 - 5 =$ ___ 29. $81 - 9 =$ ___ 30. $54 - 6 =$ ___

Name _____

# Combine Solid Figures

Name the solid figures used to make each object.

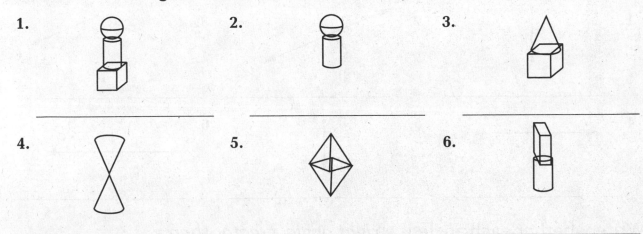

1.

2.

3.

4.

5.

6.

_____ _____ _____

_____ _____ _____

Each pair of objects should be the same. Name the solid
figure that is missing.

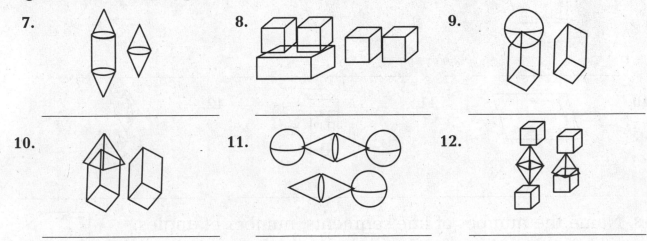

7.

8.

9.

_____ _____ _____

10.

11.

12.

_____ _____ _____

## Mixed Review

Round to the nearest ten.

13. 431 _____  14. 7,897 _____  15. 25,005 _____  16. 19,999 _____

Name the place-value position of the underlined digit.

17. 1,2̲98  18. 10̲,118  19. 900,255̲  20. 2̲43,611

_____ _____ _____ _____

© Harcourt

Name _____

# Line Segments and Angles

Name each figure.

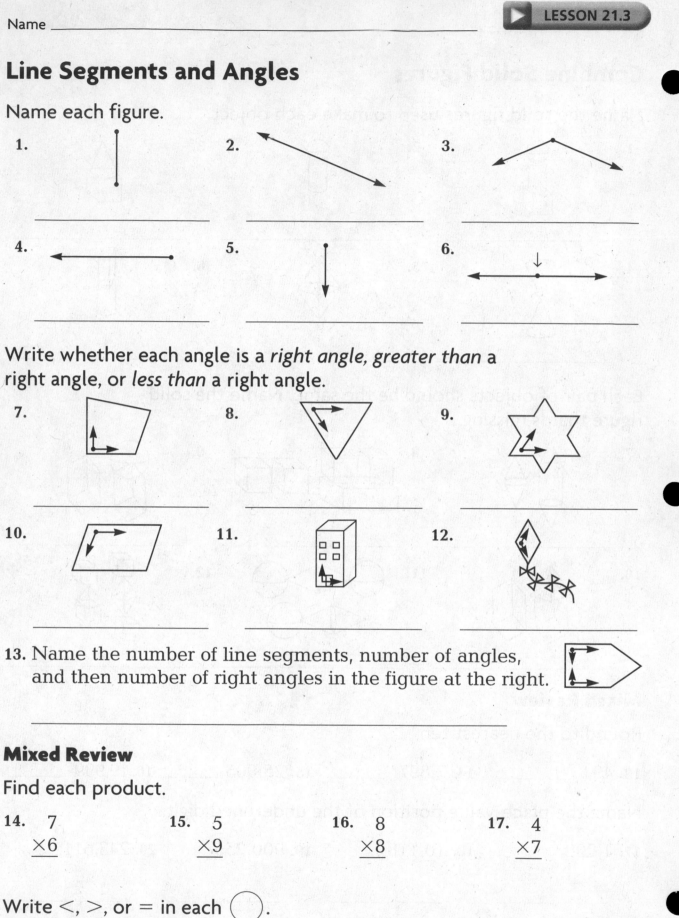

1. _____

2. _____

3. _____

4. _____

5. _____

6. _____

Write whether each angle is a *right angle, greater than* a
right angle, or *less than* a right angle.

7. _____

8. _____

9. _____

10. _____

11. _____

12. _____

13. Name the number of line segments, number of angles,
and then number of right angles in the figure at the right.

_____

## Mixed Review

Find each product.

14.     7
     $\times 6$

15.    5
     $\times 9$

16.    8
     $\times 8$

17.    4
     $\times 7$

Write $<$, $>$, or $=$ in each ◯.

18. $8 + 9$ ◯ $8 \times 9$

19. $24 + 16 + 52$ ◯ $10 \times 9$

**PW108** Practice

© Harcourt

Name _____

## Types of Lines

Describe the lines. Write *parallel* or *intersecting*.

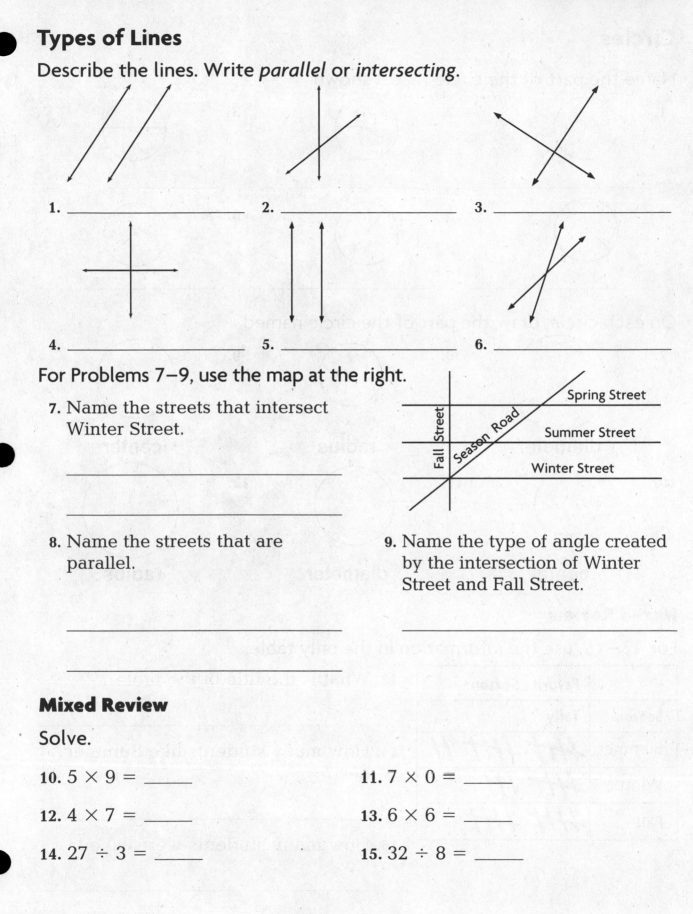

1. _____  2. _____  3. _____

4. _____  5. _____  6. _____

For Problems 7–9, use the map at the right.

7. Name the streets that intersect
   Winter Street.

   _____

   _____

8. Name the streets that are
   parallel.

   _____

   _____

9. Name the type of angle created
   by the intersection of Winter
   Street and Fall Street.

   _____

   _____

## Mixed Review

Solve.

10. $5 \times 9 =$ _____          11. $7 \times 0 =$ _____

12. $4 \times 7 =$ _____          13. $6 \times 6 =$ _____

14. $27 \div 3 =$ _____          15. $32 \div 8 =$ _____

# Circles

Name the part of the circle that is shown.

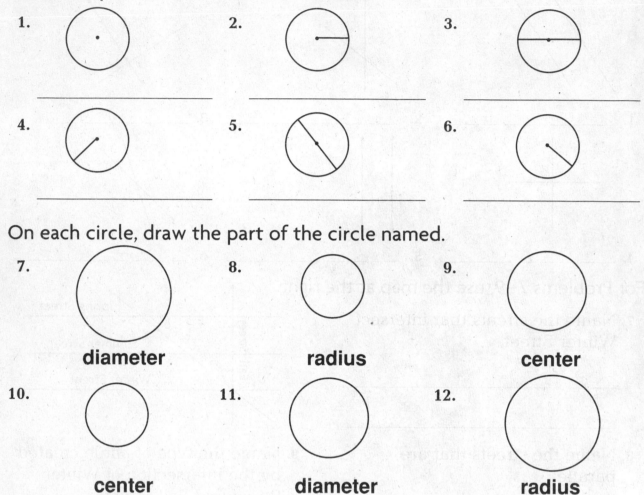

1. _____

2. _____

3. _____

4. _____

5. _____

6. _____

On each circle, draw the part of the circle named.

7.

**diameter**

8.

**radius**

9.

**center**

10.

**center**

11.

**diameter**

12.

**radius**

## Mixed Review

For 13–15, use the information in the tally table.

|  | **Favorite Season** |
|---|---|
| **Season** | **Tally** |
| Summer | ┼┼┼┼ ┼┼┼┼ ‖ |
| Winter | ┼┼┼┼ ‖‖ |
| Fall | ┼┼┼┼ ┼┼┼┼ |

13. What is the title of the table?

_____

14. How many students like Summer best?

_____

15. How many students were asked?

_____

Name _____

# Problem Solving Strategy

## Break Problems into Simpler Parts

Break problems into simpler parts to solve.

1. Paul has a wooden cube that has the design shown below carved on each of its faces. How many rays are on all the faces of the cube?

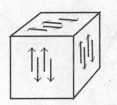

_____

2. The shoe box below has the company logo on each side. How many circles are on the box?

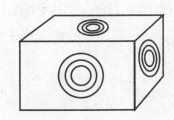

_____

3. Miranda has a toy that is the shape of a cube. The toy has the design shown below painted on the faces of the cube. How many squares are on the toy?

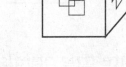

_____

4. The paper weight shown below has the same design on 4 sides. How many triangles are drawn on the paper weight?

_____

## Mixed Review

Use the grid at the right. Write the letter of the point named by the ordered pair.

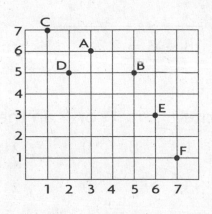

5. (7,1) _____

6. (5,5) _____

7. (1,7) _____

8. (2,5) _____

9. (3,6) _____

10. (6,3) _____

© Harcourt

**Practice   PW111**

# Polygons

Tell if each figure is a polygon. Write *yes* or *no*.

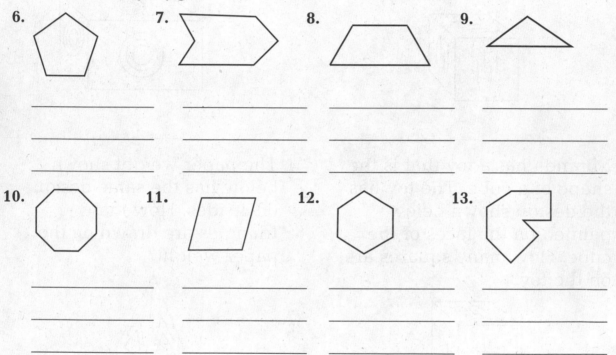

1. _____  2. _____  3. _____  4. _____  5. _____

Write the number of sides and angles each polygon has.
Then name the polygon.

6. _____  7. _____  8. _____  9. _____

_____  _____  _____  _____

10. _____  11. _____  12. _____  13. _____

_____  _____  _____  _____

_____  _____  _____  _____

## Mixed Review

Decide if the number sentence is true or false. Write *true* or *false*.

14. $18 - 6 = 12$        15. $14 + 3 = 27$        16. $7 \times 6 = 42$

_____          _____          _____

17. $18 \div 6 = 2$        18. $5 \times 7 = 12$        19. $36 \div 6 = 6$

_____          _____          _____

Write $+$, $-$, $\div$, or $\times$ in the ◯ to make the number sentence true.

20. $11 \bigcirc 8 = 19$        21. $24 \bigcirc 8 = 3$        22. $9 \bigcirc 9 = 81$

23. $35 \bigcirc 5 = 30$        24. $11 \bigcirc 7 = 77$        25. $42 \bigcirc 21 = 21$

# Congruence and Symmetry

Tell whether the two figures are congruent. Write *yes* or *no*.

1. □ ○      2. △ △      3. □ □

_____     _____     _____

4.       5.       6.

_____     _____     _____

How many lines of symmetry does each figure have?

7.    8.    9.    10.    11.

_____   _____   _____   _____   _____

## Mixed Review

Solve.

12.  $\begin{array}{r} 500 \\ -\ 47 \\ \hline \end{array}$    13.  $\begin{array}{r} 300 \\ -\ 82 \\ \hline \end{array}$    14.  $\begin{array}{r} 200 \\ -153 \\ \hline \end{array}$    15.  $\begin{array}{r} 800 \\ -237 \\ \hline \end{array}$

16.  $\begin{array}{r} 800 \\ -538 \\ \hline \end{array}$    17.  $\begin{array}{r} 100 \\ -\ 36 \\ \hline \end{array}$    18.  $\begin{array}{r} 300 \\ -\ 42 \\ \hline \end{array}$    19.  $\begin{array}{r} 700 \\ -515 \\ \hline \end{array}$

20.  $\begin{array}{r} 122 \\ 54 \\ +106 \\ \hline \end{array}$   21.  $\begin{array}{r} 682 \\ 124 \\ +589 \\ \hline \end{array}$   22.  $\begin{array}{r} 375 \\ 439 \\ +\ 86 \\ \hline \end{array}$   23.  $\begin{array}{r} 514 \\ 100 \\ +300 \\ \hline \end{array}$   24.  $\begin{array}{r} 24 \\ 315 \\ +\ \ 7 \\ \hline \end{array}$

25.  $\begin{array}{r} 8 \\ \times 3 \\ \hline \end{array}$   26.  $\begin{array}{r} 7 \\ \times 5 \\ \hline \end{array}$   27.  $\begin{array}{r} 9 \\ \times 7 \\ \hline \end{array}$   28.  $\begin{array}{r} 11 \\ \times 6 \\ \hline \end{array}$   29.  $\begin{array}{r} 10 \\ \times 8 \\ \hline \end{array}$

Name _____

# Combine Plane Figures

Tell if each figure will tessellate. Write *yes* or *no*.

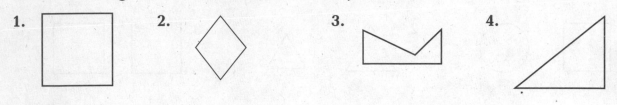

1. _____    2. _____    3. _____    4. _____

Trace and cut out each figure. Use each figure to make a tessellation.
You may color your design.

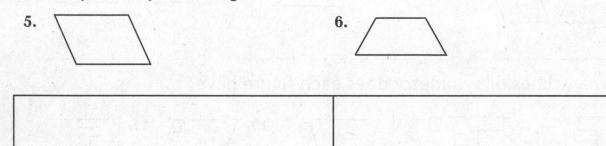

5.       6.

## Mixed Review

Write each number in standard form.

**7.** 20,000 + 800 + 5    **8.** 30,000 + 6,000 + 10    **9.** 50,000 + 7,000 + 3

_____    _____    _____

Estimate each sum.

| **10.** | **11.** | **12.** | **13.** | **14.** |
|---|---|---|---|---|
| 874 | 952 | 892 | 352 | 925 |
| + 635 | + 411 | + 999 | + 429 | + 659 |

Write the number of sides and angles each plane figure has.

**15.** hexagon      **16.** octagon      **17.** pentagon

_____      _____      _____

© Harcourt

Name _____

Name _____

# Problem Solving Strategy

**Find a Pattern**

Find a pattern to solve.

1. Sarah is gluing shapes around a frame. Draw the next three shapes in her pattern.

 ___ ___ ___

2. Jeff is decorating the border of a crown. Draw the next three shapes in his pattern.

○ • ● ○ ○ • ● ○ ○ ___ ___

3. There is a pattern in the numbers below. What will the next two numbers be?

3, 14, 25, 36, ____, ____

4. Sketch the next two dot triangles to continue the pattern below.

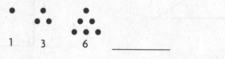 _____

5. Julio drew this pattern on his paper. What is the next figure in the pattern?

△ □ ◇ ⬡ △ □ ? _____

6. Maria writes this number pattern:

5, 14, 23, 32, 41

Describe Maria's number pattern.

_____

## Mixed Review

Write the rule and the next number in each pattern.

7. 10, 15, 20, 25, __?__   8. 3, 6, 9, 12, 15, __?__   9. 56, 50, 44, 38, __?__

Find the product.

10. $6 \times 6 =$ ____   11. $4 \times 6 =$ ____   12. $8 \times 6 =$ ____

13. $5 \times 5 =$ ____   14. $5 \times 8 =$ ____   15. $5 \times 7 =$ ____

## Triangles

Write if each angle is a *right angle, greater than* a right
angle, or *less than* a right angle.

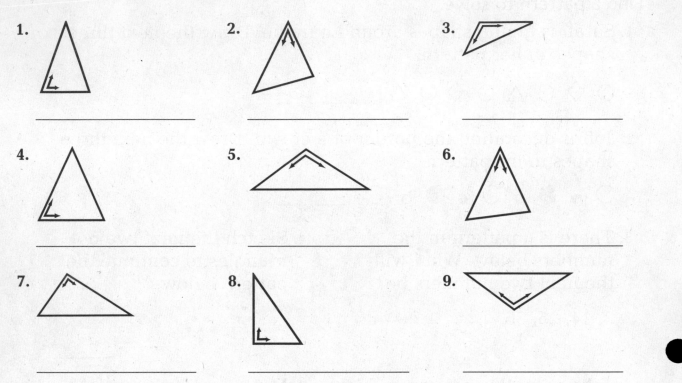

1. _____

2. _____

3. _____

4. _____

5. _____

6. _____

7. _____

8. _____

9. _____

## Mixed Review

Tell whether the two figures are congruent. Write *yes or no.*

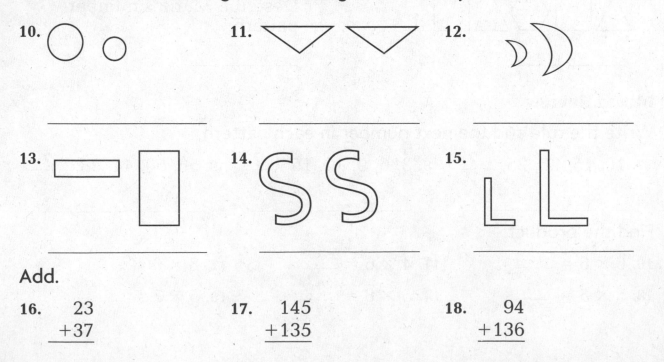

10. _____

11. _____

12. _____

13. _____

14. _____

15. _____

Add.

16.  23
   +37

17.  145
   +135

18.  94
   +136

## Sort Triangles

For 1–3, use the triangles at the right. Write *A*, *B*, or *C*.

1. Which triangle is scalene? _____

2. Which triangles have at least
   2 equal sides? _____

3. Which triangle has 1 angle that
   is greater than a right angle? _____

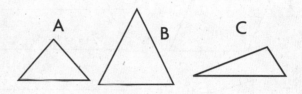

For 4–7, write one letter from each box to describe each triangle.

| | |
|---|---|
| **a.** Equilateral | **d.** It has 1 right angle. |
| **b.** Isosceles | **e.** It has 1 angle greater than a right angle. |
| **c.** Scalene | **f.** All angles are less than a right angle. |

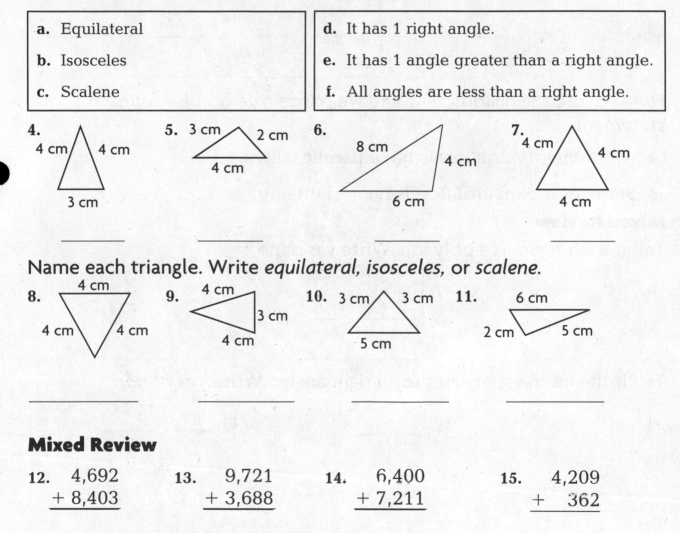

4.  4 cm  4 cm  3 cm _____

5.  3 cm  2 cm  4 cm _____

6.  8 cm  4 cm  6 cm _____

7.  4 cm  4 cm  4 cm _____

Name each triangle. Write *equilateral, isosceles,* or *scalene.*

8.  4 cm  4 cm  4 cm _____

9.  4 cm  3 cm  4 cm _____

10.  3 cm  3 cm  5 cm _____

11.  6 cm  2 cm  5 cm _____

## Mixed Review

12.  4,692
    + 8,403

13.  9,721
    + 3,688

14.  6,400
    + 7,211

15.  4,209
    +  362

Name _____

## Quadrilaterals

Describe the angles and sides of each quadrilateral.

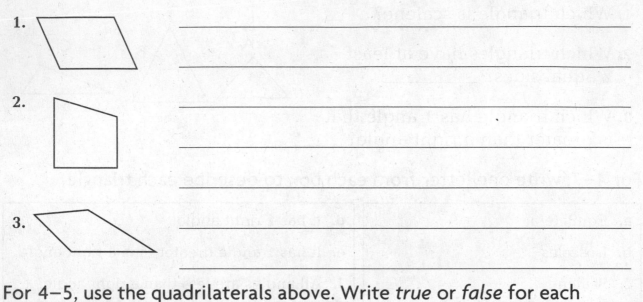

1. _____

   _____

2. _____

   _____

   _____

3. _____

   _____

For 4–5, use the quadrilaterals above. Write *true* or *false* for each statement.

4. All of the quadrilaterals have parallel sides. _____

5. Some of the quadrilaterals have right angles. _____

## Mixed Review

Tell if each figure is a polygon. Write *yes* or *no*.

6.

7.

8.

_____     _____     _____

Tell if the intersecting lines form right angles. Write *yes* or *no*.

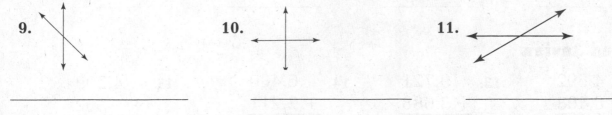

9.

10.

11.

_____     _____     _____

Divide.

12. $9 \div 3 =$ _____     13. $72 \div 9 =$ _____     14. $48 \div 6 =$ _____

15. $54 \div 6 =$ _____     16. $49 \div 7 =$ _____     17. $32 \div 8 =$ _____

**PW118  Practice**

Name _____

## Sort Quadrilaterals

For 1–3, use the quadrilaterals below. Write *A, B, C, D,* or *E.*

1. Which quadrilaterals have 2 pairs of equal sides? _____

2. Which quadrilaterals have no right angles? _____

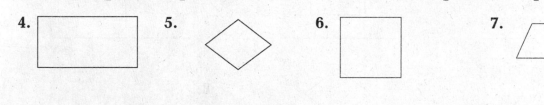

3. How are quadrilaterals A and B alike? How are they different?

_____

_____

_____

For 4–7, write *all* the letters that describe each quadrilateral. Then write a name for each quadrilateral.

**a.** It has 4 equal sides.

**b.** It has 2 pairs of parallel sides.

**c.** It has 4 right angles.

**d.** It has 2 pairs of equal sides.

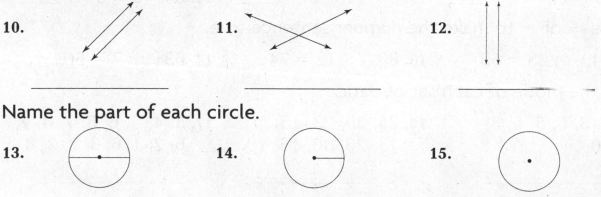

_____     _____     _____     _____

_____     _____

## Mixed Review

8. 3 + 3 + 3 + 3 + 3 + 3 = _____     9. 7 + 7 + 7 + 7 + 7 + 7 = _____

Describe the lines. Write *intersecting* or *parallel.*

10.          11.          12.

_____     _____     _____

Name the part of each circle.

13.          14.          15.

_____          _____          _____

Name _____

## Problem Solving Skill
## Identify Relationships

1. What are all the ways to name the polygon below? What is the best name for the polygon?

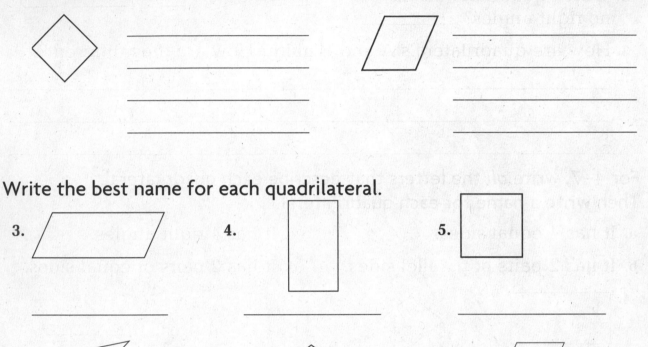

2. What are all the ways to name the polygon below? What is the best name for the polygon?

_____
_____
_____

_____
_____
_____

Write the best name for each quadrilateral.

3. _____

4. _____

5. _____

6. _____

7. _____

8. _____

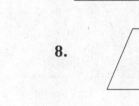

## Mixed Review
Solve.

9. $(8 \times 2) \times 0 =$ _____   10. $3 \times (4 \times 2) =$ _____   11. $6 \times (3 \times 3) =$ _____

Write + or − to make the number sentence true.

12. 44 ◯ 25 = 69     13. 86 ◯ 12 = 74     14. 63 ◯ 7 = 56

Find the mode of each set of data.

15. 2, 3, 5, 5, 6, 8, 10, 5

16. 25, 29, 23, 15, 13, 26, 30, 15, 19

17. 3, 4, 2, 6, 3, 7, 4, 2, 6, 2, 4, 6, 3, 7, 3, 8, 1

_____     _____     _____

© Harcourt

Name _____

# Length

Estimate the length in inches. Then use a ruler to
measure to the nearest inch.

|  | Estimate | Measure |
|---|---|---|

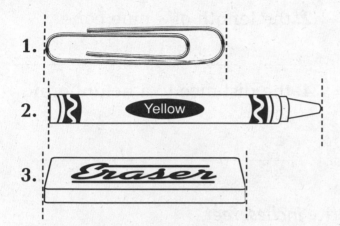

1. _____ _____

2. Yellow _____ _____

3. *Eraser* _____ _____

Measure the length to the nearest half inch.

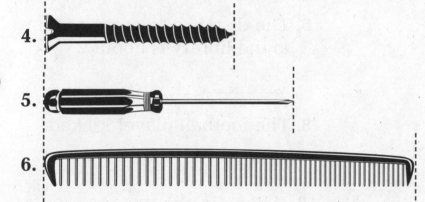

4. _____

5. _____

6. _____

## Mixed Review

For 7–11, use the solid figure at the right.

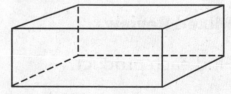

7. How many faces does the solid figure have?

8. How many edges does the solid figure have?

_____ _____

9. How many faces of the solid figure are not squares?

10. How many faces of the solid figure are squares?

11. What is the name of the solid figure above?

_____ _____ _____

**Practice   PW121**

© Harcourt

# Inch, Foot, Yard, and Mile

Choose the unit you would use to measure each.
Write *inch*, *foot*, *yard*, or *mile*.

**1.** the length of a table

_____

**2.** the length of a pine cone

_____

**3.** the length of a driveway

_____

**4.** the distance to a neighboring town

_____

Choose the best unit of measure. Write *inches*, *feet*, *yards*, or *miles*.

**5.** A pencil is about

5 _____ long.

**6.** The distance from your home to the library is about 2

_____.

**7.** A bike is about

4 _____ long.

**8.** The football player kicked

the ball 45 _____.

**9.** Peter grew almost

2 _____ in one year.

**10.** A man is about

6 _____ tall.

## Mixed Review

Find each product.

**11.** $7 \times 2 =$ _____

**12.** _____ $= 9 \times 5$

**13.** $6 \times 6 =$ _____

Find each quotient.

**14.** $14 \div 2 =$ _____

**15.** $27 \div 3 =$ _____

**16.** _____ $= 18 \div 6$

**17.** $24 \div 6 =$ _____

**18.** _____ $= 20 \div 4$

**19.** $8 \div 4 =$ _____

Name _____

LESSON 24.3

# Capacity

Circle the better estimate.

1.

10 quarts or 10 gallons

2.

2 cups or 2 quarts

Compare. Write <, >, or = in each ◯.

3. 3 cups ◯ 1 pint

4. 1 gallon ◯ 4 quarts

5. 3 pints ◯ 2 quarts

6. 1 gallon ◯ 10 cups

7. 7 pints ◯ 1 gallon

8. 2 gallons ◯ 16 pints

# Mixed Review

9. 6
   × 8

10. 9
    × 9

11. 86
    − 51

12. 99
    − 83

13. 7)63

14. 5)40

15. 6)24

16. 1)12

17. Find the sum of 862 and 137.

_____

18. Find the product of 6 and 9.

_____

19. Which number is greater: 736 or 763?

_____

20. What is 56 ÷ 8?

_____

21. Find the difference of 789 and 326.

_____

22. What is 16 ÷ 8?

_____

© Harcourt

**Practice   PW123**

# Weight

Choose the unit you would use to weigh each.
Write *ounce* or *pound*.

1.

_____

2.

_____

3.

_____

4.

_____

5.

_____

6.

_____

Circle the better estimate.

7.

4 pounds or
4 ounces

8.

10 ounces or
10 pounds

9.

10 pounds or
10 ounces

## Mixed Review

Order each group of numbers from least to greatest.

10. 234, 561, 144 _____

11. 899, 998, 989 _____

12. 1,482; 1,248; 1,842 _____

13. 6,479; 8,372; 8,362 _____

Write the missing factor.

14. $4 \times$ _____ $= 16$

15. $12 = 6 \times$ _____

16. $3 \times$ _____ $= 27$

17. $80 =$ _____ $\times 8$

18. _____ $\times 3 = 33$

19. $487 =$ _____ $\times 487$

# Ways to Change Units

Complete. Use the Table of Measures to help.

**1.** Change yards to feet.

larger unit _____

1 yard = _____

**2.** Change quarts to gallons.

larger unit _____

1 gallon = _____

Change the units. Use the Table of Measures to help.

**3.** _____ pints = 1 quart

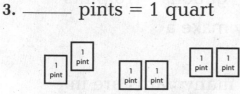

_____ pints = 5 quarts

**4.** _____ inches = 1 foot

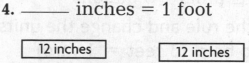

_____ inches = 6 feet

**5.** _____ cups = 1 quart

| cups | 4 | 8 | 12 | 16 |
|-------|---|---|----|----|
| quarts | 1 | 2 | 3 | 4 |

_____ cups = 3 quarts

**6.** _____ feet = 1 yard

| feet | 3 | 6 | 9 | 12 |
|-------|---|---|---|----|
| yards | 1 | 2 | 3 | 4 |

_____ feet = 4 yards

## Mixed Review

Multiply.

**7.** $8 \times 9 =$ _____

**8.** $10 \times 4 =$ _____

**9.** $6 \times 7 =$ _____

Divide.

**10.** $18 \div 9 =$ _____

**11.** $36 \div 4 =$ _____

**12.** $40 \div 8 =$ _____

Add.

**13.** $15 + 13 + 11 =$ _____

**14.** $35 + 9 + 15 =$ _____

**15.** $27 + 13 + 48 =$ _____

Subtract.

**16.** $15 - 13 =$ _____

**17.** $83 - 17 =$ _____

**18.** $57 - 48 =$ _____

# Algebra: Rules for Changing Units

Use the rules to change the units. (8 pints = 1 gallon)

**1.** How many pints are in 3 gallons?

Rule: Multiply the number of gallons by 8.

$3 \times 8 =$ _____

_____ pints = 3 gallons

**2.** How many gallons are in 16 pints?

Rule: Divide the number of pints by 8.

$16 \div 8 =$ _____

_____ gallons = 16 pints

Write the rule and change the units. You may make a table to help. (3 feet = 1 yard)

**3.** How many feet are in 8 yards?

Rule: _____ the number of yards by 3.

$8 \times 3 =$ _____

_____ feet = 8 yards

**4.** How many yards are in 15 feet?

Rule: _____ the number of feet by 3.

$15 \div 3 =$ _____

_____ yards = 15 feet

**5.** How many yards are in 21 feet?

Rule:

_____

_____

_____ yards = 21 feet

**6.** How many feet are in 10 yards?

Rule:

_____

_____

_____ feet = 10 yards

## Mixed Review

Use a ruler to measure to the nearest inch.

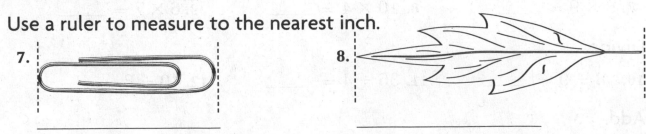

**7.** _____

**8.** _____

Choose the unit you would use to measure each. Write *inch, foot, yard,* or *mile.*

**9.** length of a school bus

_____

**10.** length of a scissors

_____

© Harcourt

# Problem Solving Skill

## Use a Graph

For 1–4, use the graphs.

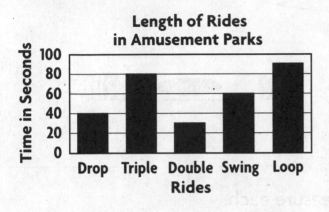

**Length of Rides in Amusement Parks**

| Magazines Sold | |
|---|---|
| Shirley | 🕮🕮 🕮🕮 🕮🕮 🕮🕮 🕮🕮 |
| Fred | 🕮🕮 🕮🕮 🕮🕮 . |
| Morton | 🕮🕮 🕮🕮 |
| Amber | 🕮🕮 🕮🕮 🕮🕮 🕮🕮 🕮🕮 🕮🕮 . |
| Mack | 🕮🕮 🕮🕮 🕮🕮 🕮🕮 🕮🕮 🕮🕮 🕮🕮 🕮🕮 🕮🕮 🕮🕮 |
| Marsha | 🕮🕮 |

Key: Each 🕮🕮 = 2 magazines.

**1.** Which ride lasts the longest? the shortest?

_____

**2.** How long would you ride if you went on Swing, and twice on Triple?

_____

**3.** How many magazines did Fred sell?

_____

**4.** How many more magazines did Amber sell than Morton?

_____

## Mixed Review

**5.** $(1 \times 6) \times 8 =$ _____

**6.** $(3 \times 2) \times 4 =$ _____

**7.** $9 \times (3 \times 3) =$ _____

**8.** $5 \times (2 \times 5) =$ _____

**9.** $2 + 4 + 9 =$ _____

**10.** $8 + 7 + 2 =$ _____

**11.** $6 + 3 + 8 =$ _____

**12.** $5 + 1 + 4 =$ _____

**13.** $(8 \times 8) \times 2 =$ _____

**14.** $(4 \times 6) \times 2 =$ _____

**15.** $5 + 10 + 16 =$ _____

**16.** $8 + 4 + 5 =$ _____

# Length

Estimate the length in centimeters. Then use a ruler to measure to the nearest centimeter.

1. 

_____

2. 

_____

3. 

_____

Choose the unit you would use to measure each.
Write *cm, m,* or *km*.

4. the length of your little finger

_____

5. the distance between 2 towns

_____

6. the width of a chalkboard

_____

7. the length of your math book

_____

8. the length of the Mississippi River

_____

9. the distance between your house and your neighbor's house

_____

## Mixed Review

10. $3.68
 − $1.79

11. 752
 + 134

12. $54 \div$ _____ $= 6$

13. $8 \times 0 =$ _____

14. $5 \div$ _____ $= 5$

15. $7 \times$ _____ $= 56$

Find the pattern and solve.

16. 64, 56, 48, _____, 32, _____

17. 1, 3, 5, 7, 9, 11, _____

# Problem Solving Strategy

## Make a Table

Complete this table.

1.

| Meters | 1 | 2 | 3 | | | | | | |
|---|---|---|---|---|---|---|---|---|---|
| Centimeters | 100 | 200 | | | | | | | |

For 2–3, use the completed table above.

2. Gary needs 500 centimeters of space for a bookcase. How many meters of space does he need?

_____

3. Kara needs 9 meters of string. How many centimeters of string does she need?

_____

Jake drew a line that was 3 decimeters long. How many centimeters long was his line?

4. Which table helps solve the problem? _____

A
| Kilometers | 1 | 2 | 3 |
|---|---|---|---|
| Meters | 1,000 | 2,000 | 3,000 |

C
| Centimeters | 100 | 200 | 300 |
|---|---|---|---|
| Meters | 1 | 2 | 3 |

B
| Meters | 1 | 2 | 3 |
|---|---|---|---|
| Decimeters | 10 | 20 | 30 |

D
| Decimeters | 1 | 2 | 3 |
|---|---|---|---|
| Centimeters | 10 | 20 | 30 |

5. What is the solution to the problem? _____

## Mixed Review

Draw the next 3 shapes in the pattern.

6. ▽ □ △ □ ▽ □ △ □ ▽ □ △ □ _____

7. ○ ○ □ □ ○ ○ □ ○ ○ □ _____

Name _____

# Capacity: Liters and Milliliters

Circle the better estimate.

1.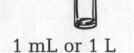

    1 mL or 1 L

2.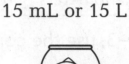

    4 mL or 4 L

3.

    15 mL or 15 L

4.

    250 mL or 250 L

5.

    2 mL or 2 L

6.

    3,000 mL or 3,000 L

Choose the unit you would use to measure each.
Write *mL* or *L*.

7. a mug of hot
   chocolate

   _____

8. water in a
   swimming pool

   _____

9. a glass of juice

   _____

10. water for a flower
    garden

    _____

11. a can of soup

    _____

12. 5 pitchers of
    lemonade

    _____

## Mixed Review

13. $59 + 64 + 93 =$ _____

14. $726 - 493 =$ _____

Write $<$, $>$, or $=$ in each $\bigcirc$.

15. $7 \times 8 \bigcirc 87 - 31$

16. $56 \div 7 \bigcirc 3 \times 2$

17. $40 \div 8 \bigcirc 7$

18. $9 \times 4 \bigcirc 12 \times 3$

Continue each pattern.

19. 8, 16, 24, 32, _____

20. 4, 9, 14, 19, _____, _____

# Mass: Grams and Kilograms

Circle the better estimate.

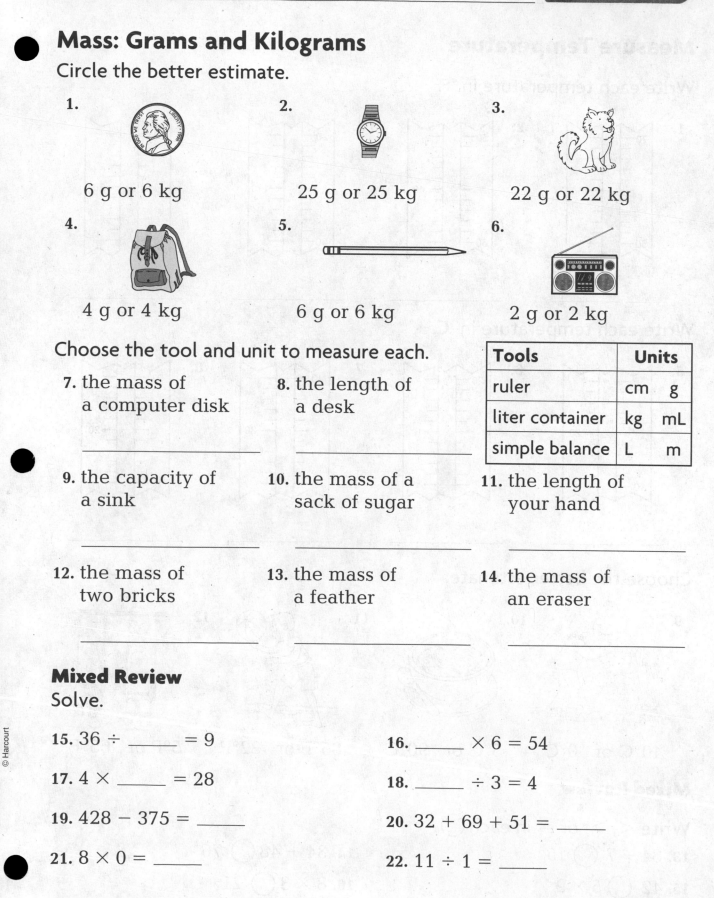

1.

6 g or 6 kg

2.

25 g or 25 kg

3.

22 g or 22 kg

4.

4 g or 4 kg

5.

6 g or 6 kg

6.

2 g or 2 kg

Choose the tool and unit to measure each.

| Tools | Units | |
|---|---|---|
| ruler | cm | g |
| liter container | kg | mL |
| simple balance | L | m |

7. the mass of
a computer disk

_____

8. the length of
a desk

_____

9. the capacity of
a sink

_____

10. the mass of a
sack of sugar

_____

11. the length of
your hand

_____

12. the mass of
two bricks

_____

13. the mass of
a feather

_____

14. the mass of
an eraser

_____

## Mixed Review
Solve.

15. $36 \div$ _____ $= 9$

16. _____ $\times 6 = 54$

17. $4 \times$ _____ $= 28$

18. _____ $\div 3 = 4$

19. $428 - 375 =$ _____

20. $32 + 69 + 51 =$ _____

21. $8 \times 0 =$ _____

22. $11 \div 1 =$ _____

# Measure Temperature

Write each temperature in °F.

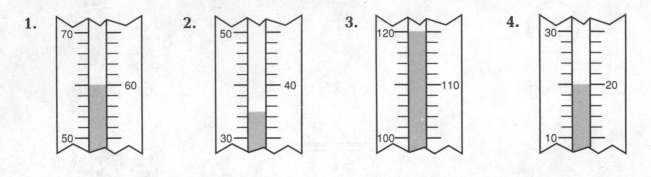

1. _____  2. _____  3. _____  4. _____

Write each temperature in °C.

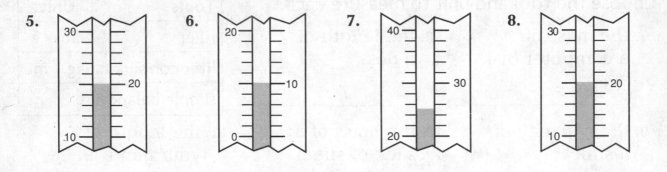

5. _____  6. _____  7. _____  8. _____

Choose the better estimate.

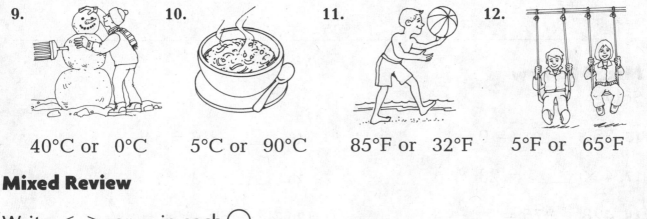

9. 40°C or 0°C

10. 5°C or 90°C

11. 85°F or 32°F

12. 5°F or 65°F

## Mixed Review

Write <, >, or = in each ◯.

13. 84 ÷ 7 ◯ 15

14. 34 + 48 ◯ 76

15. 42 ◯ 5 × 9

16. 8 × 3 ◯ 21

Name _____

# Perimeter

## Vocabulary

Fill in the blank to complete the sentence.

1. The distance around a figure is its _____.

---

Find the perimeter of each figure.

2.

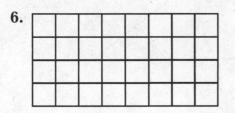

_____

3.

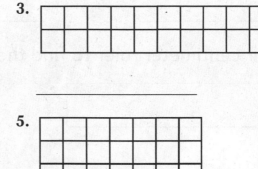

_____

4.

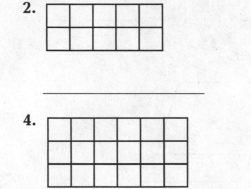

_____

5.

_____

6.

_____

7.

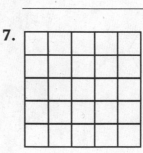

_____

## Mixed Review

8.
$$\begin{array}{r} 716 \\ -\ 304 \\ \hline \end{array}$$

9.
$$\begin{array}{r} 241 \\ +\ \ 93 \\ \hline \end{array}$$

10.
$$\begin{array}{r} 876 \\ -\ 759 \\ \hline \end{array}$$

11. $8\overline{)56}$

12. $9\overline{)72}$

13. $8\overline{)64}$

14. $7\overline{)28}$

15. $6\overline{)42}$

16. $7\overline{)35}$

# Estimate and Find Perimeter

Find the perimeter.

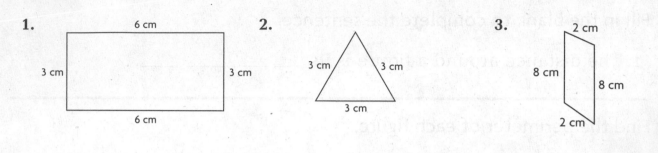

1. 6 cm / 3 cm / 3 cm / 6 cm

2.  3 cm / 3 cm / 3 cm

3.  2 cm / 8 cm / 8 cm / 2 cm

_____     _____     _____

Use your centimeter ruler to find the perimeter.

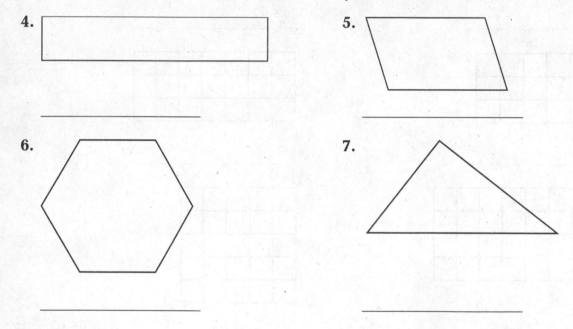

4.

_____

5.

_____

6.

_____

7.

_____

## Mixed Review

Use the graph.

8. How many students chose blue as their favorite color?

_____

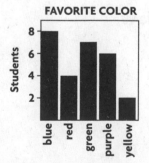

**FAVORITE COLOR**

Students

8
6
4
2

blue  red  green  purple  yellow

9. How many more students chose green than yellow?

_____

10. How many students voted in all?

_____

# Area of Plane Figures

Find the area of each rectangle. Write the area in square units.

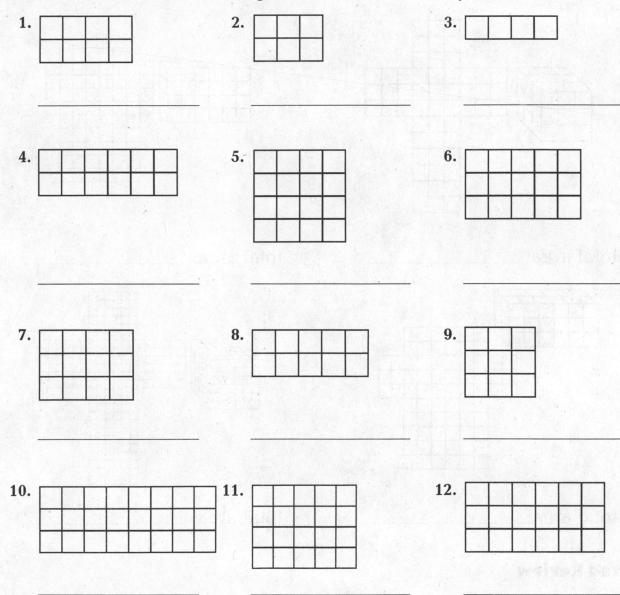

1.

_____

2.

_____

3.

_____

4.

_____

5.

_____

6.

_____

7.

_____

8.

_____

9.

_____

10.

_____

11.

_____

12.

_____

## Mixed Review

Find each missing number.

13. $4 + \_\_\_ = 11$

14. $5 + \_\_\_ = 8$

15. $9 + \_\_\_ = 17$

16. $2 + \_\_\_ = 10$

17. $\_\_\_ \times 8 = 64$

18. $\_\_\_ \times 12 = 48$

# Area of Solid Figures

Find the total area that covers each solid figure.

1.

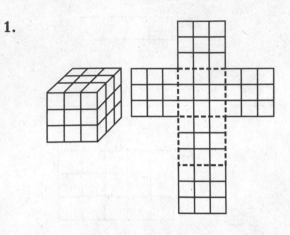

total area: _____

2.

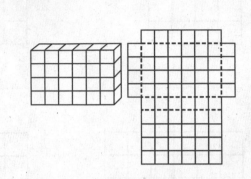

total area: _____

3.

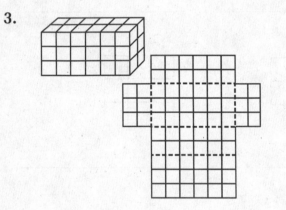

total area: _____

4.

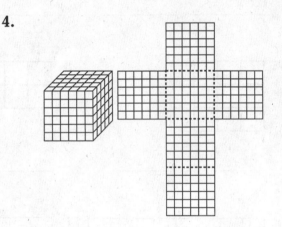

total area: _____

## Mixed Review

**Add.**

5.  $3.89
  + $5.19

6.  $3.90
  + $6.22

7.  $6.75
  + $3.81

**Subtract.**

8.  $7.20
  − $4.05

9.  $8.00
  − $4.13

10.  $9.91
  − $3.21

# Problem Solving Skill

## Make Generalizations

1. A laundry room is shaped like a rectangle. The area of the room is 6 square yards. The perimeter is 10 yards. The room is longer than it is wide. How wide is the room? How long is the room?

2. Mark has a piece of string that is 12 inches long. He shapes the string into a rectangle that encloses an area of 5 square inches. Can Mark enclose a greater area with the same string? If so, what is the area?

3. The perimeter of a table is 24 feet. The table is twice as long as it is wide. What is the table's width? length? area?

4. Mrs. Brown put a wallpaper border around a room that is 10 feet long and 9 feet wide. How long is the wallpaper border? What is the area of the room?

## Mixed Review

Solve.

5. The time shown on Mario's watch is 10:45. He has just finished raking leaves for 30 minutes. Before that, he played basketball for 1 hour. At what time did he start playing basketball?

6. Carrie is swimming in the middle lane of the pool. She waves to her father, who is swimming 3 lanes away, in the end lane. How many lanes does the pool have?

7. $\begin{array}{r} 11 \\ \times 6 \\ \hline \end{array}$    8. $\begin{array}{r} 5 \\ \times 7 \\ \hline \end{array}$    9. $\begin{array}{r} 7 \\ \times 7 \\ \hline \end{array}$    10. $\begin{array}{r} 8 \\ \times 3 \\ \hline \end{array}$    11. $\begin{array}{r} 12 \\ \times 6 \\ \hline \end{array}$

# Estimate and Find Volume

Use cubes to make each solid. Then write the volume in cubic units.

1.
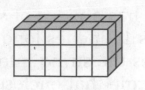

volume: _____

2.
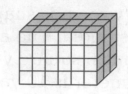

volume: _____

3.
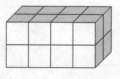

volume: _____

4.

volume: _____

Find the volume of each solid. Write the volume in cubic units.

5.
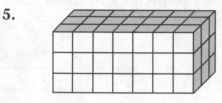

volume: _____

6.
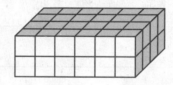

volume: _____

7.
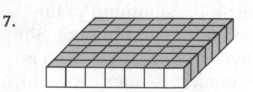

volume: _____

8.

volume: _____

## Mixed Review

Add.

9.     532
    + 196

10.    158
    + 270

11.    851
    + 653

© Harcourt

# Count Parts of a Whole

Write a fraction in numbers and words that names the shaded part.

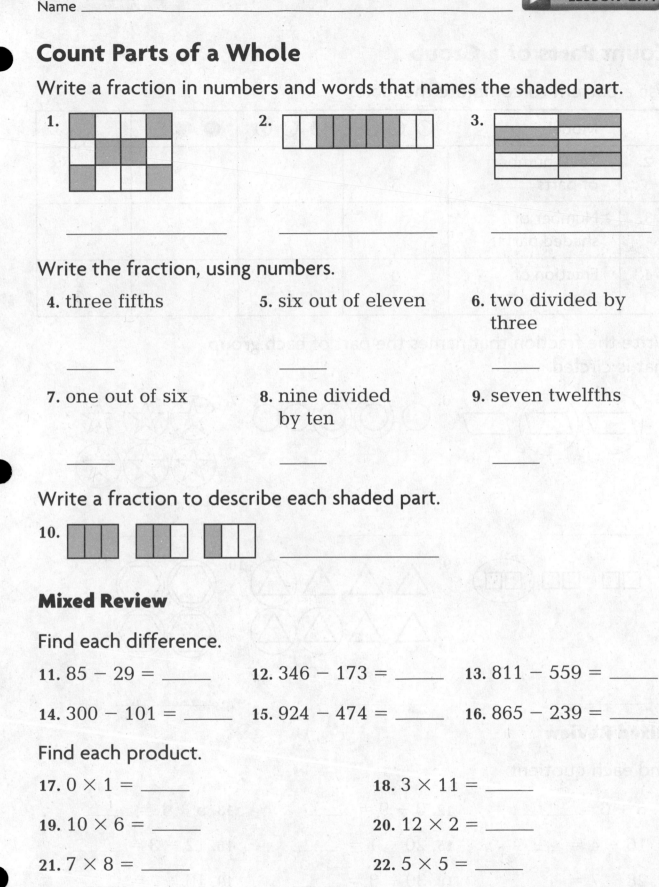

1.

2.

3.

_____     _____     _____

Write the fraction, using numbers.

4. three fifths

5. six out of eleven

6. two divided by three

_____        _____        _____

7. one out of six

8. nine divided by ten

9. seven twelfths

_____        _____        _____

Write a fraction to describe each shaded part.

10.  _____

## Mixed Review

Find each difference.

11. 85 − 29 = _____     12. 346 − 173 = _____     13. 811 − 559 = _____

14. 300 − 101 = _____     15. 924 − 474 = _____     16. 865 − 239 = _____

Find each product.

17. $0 \times 1 =$ _____        18. $3 \times 11 =$ _____

19. $10 \times 6 =$ _____        20. $12 \times 2 =$ _____

21. $7 \times 8 =$ _____        22. $5 \times 5 =$ _____

© Harcourt

Name _____

# Count Parts of a Group

Use a pattern to complete the table.

| 1. | Model | ○ ○ ○ | ● ○ ○ | ● ● ○ | |
|---|---|---|---|---|---|
| 2. | Total number of parts | 3 | | 3 | 3 |
| 3. | Number of shaded parts | | 1 | 2 | 3 |
| 4. | Fraction of shaded parts | $\frac{0}{3}$ | $\frac{1}{3}$ | | $\frac{3}{3}$ |

Write the fraction that names the part of each group that is circled.

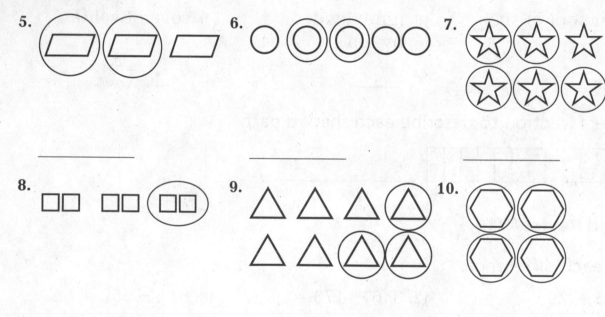

5. _____

6. _____

7. _____

8. _____

9. _____

10. _____

## Mixed Review

Find each quotient.

11. $6 \div 6 =$ _____

12. $0 \div 9 =$ _____

13. $5 \div 1 =$ _____

14. $16 \div 4 =$ _____

15. $20 \div 1 =$ _____

16. $12 \div 3 =$ _____

17. $28 \div 7 =$ _____

18. $30 \div 3 =$ _____

19. $16 \div 2 =$ _____

20. $64 \div 8 =$ _____

21. $42 \div 7 =$ _____

22. $72 \div 9 =$ _____

© Harcourt

● **Equivalent Fractions**

Find an equivalent fraction. Use fraction bars.

1. [1]
[$\frac{1}{3}$]

_____

2. [1]
[$\frac{1}{8}$ $\frac{1}{8}$ $\frac{1}{8}$ $\frac{1}{8}$ $\frac{1}{8}$ $\frac{1}{8}$]

_____

3. [1]
[$\frac{1}{8}$ $\frac{1}{8}$ $\frac{1}{8}$ $\frac{1}{8}$]

_____

4. [1]
[$\frac{1}{6}$ $\frac{1}{6}$ $\frac{1}{6}$ $\frac{1}{6}$]

_____

5. [1]
[$\frac{1}{10}$ $\frac{1}{10}$]

_____

6. [1]
[$\frac{1}{9}$ $\frac{1}{9}$ $\frac{1}{9}$ $\frac{1}{9}$ $\frac{1}{9}$ $\frac{1}{9}$]

_____

Find the missing numerator. Use fraction bars.

7. $\frac{1}{3} = \frac{\square}{6}$

8. $\frac{3}{5} = \frac{\square}{10}$

9. $\frac{3}{4} = \frac{\square}{8}$

10. $\frac{1}{10} = \frac{\square}{5}$

11. $\frac{12}{12} = \frac{\square}{6}$

12. $\frac{2}{3} = \frac{\square}{12}$

13. $\frac{6}{8} = \frac{\square}{4}$

14. $\frac{4}{5} = \frac{\square}{10}$

15. $\frac{1}{3} = \frac{\square}{9}$

16. $\frac{4}{8} = \frac{\square}{4}$

17. $\frac{3}{5} = \frac{\square}{10}$

18. $\frac{2}{12} = \frac{\square}{6}$

**Mixed Review**

Round to the nearest thousand.

19. 554 _____

20. 3,764 _____

21. 7,298 _____

22. 9,099 _____

Find the quotient.

23. $12 \div 3 =$ ____

24. $16 \div 8 =$ ____

25. $33 \div 3 =$ ____

26. $64 \div 8 =$ ____

27. $63 \div 7 =$ ____

28. $10 \div 1 =$ ____

29. $6 \div 0 =$ ____

30. $25 \div 5 =$ ____

31. $72 \div 8 =$ ____

32. $32 \div 4 =$ ____

33. $45 \div 5 =$ ____

34. $48 \div 6 =$ ____

Name _____

# Compare and Order Fractions

Compare. Write <, >, or = in each ◯.

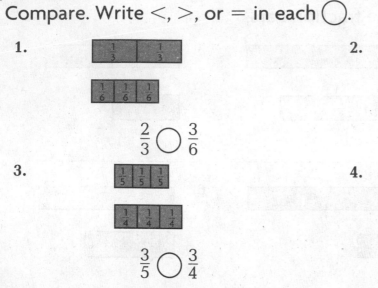

1.

$\frac{2}{3}$ ◯ $\frac{3}{6}$

2.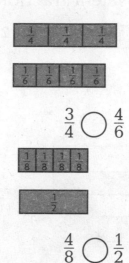

$\frac{3}{4}$ ◯ $\frac{4}{6}$

3.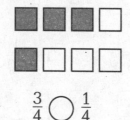

$\frac{3}{5}$ ◯ $\frac{3}{4}$

4.

$\frac{4}{8}$ ◯ $\frac{1}{2}$

Compare the part of each group that is shaded. Write < or > in each ◯.

5.

$\frac{3}{4}$ ◯ $\frac{1}{4}$

6.

$\frac{5}{8}$ ◯ $\frac{7}{8}$

7. Order $\frac{1}{2}$, $\frac{2}{3}$, and $\frac{3}{4}$ from greatest to least.

_____

8. Order $\frac{1}{8}$, $\frac{1}{3}$, and $\frac{3}{6}$ from greatest to least.

_____

## Mixed Review

Compare. Write <, >, or = in each ◯.

9. 472 ◯ 619

10. 3,009 ◯ 2,588

11. 820 ◯ 820

Order each set of numbers from least to greatest.

12. 35, 63, 17

13. 200, 199, 205

14. 484, 848, 488

_____

_____

_____

# Problem Solving Strategy

## Make A Model

Use *make a model* to solve.

1. Sean spent $\frac{2}{10}$ of his allowance on a book and $\frac{2}{5}$ on a baseball. On which item did he spend more?

_____

2. Alex read $\frac{3}{8}$ of a book. Joel read $\frac{1}{2}$ of the same book. Who read more?

_____

3. Mr. Ruiz made a divider for his patio. He used 9 stacks of bricks with 7 bricks in each stack. How many bricks did he use?

_____

4. The border in Shea's room repeats square, triangle, triangle, circle. If one wall has 9 repeats, how many triangles are on that wall?

_____

## Mixed Review

5. Tia, Juan, and Carla are standing in a line. Tia is behind Juan. Carla is in front of Juan. In what order are they standing?

_____

6. There are 67 marbles in a jar. Ed takes out 22 marbles on Monday. On Tuesday, Ed puts 35 marbles into the jar. How many marbles are in the jar now?

_____

Complete.

7. 3 feet = __?__ yard

8. 1 ft = __?__ in.

9. 1 gallon = __?__ quarts

_____ _____ _____

10. 15, 10, 5, ____

11. 24, 26, 28, 30, ____

12. 17, 20, 23, ____

# Add Fractions

Find the sum.

1.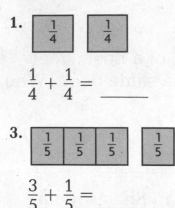

$\frac{1}{4} + \frac{1}{4} =$ _____

2.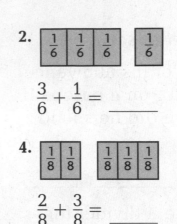

$\frac{3}{6} + \frac{1}{6} =$ _____

3. $\boxed{\frac{1}{5}}\boxed{\frac{1}{5}}\boxed{\frac{1}{5}}\ \boxed{\frac{1}{5}}$

$\frac{3}{5} + \frac{1}{5} =$ _____

4. $\boxed{\frac{1}{8}}\boxed{\frac{1}{8}}\ \boxed{\frac{1}{8}}\boxed{\frac{1}{8}}\boxed{\frac{1}{8}}$

$\frac{2}{8} + \frac{3}{8} =$ _____

Use fraction bars to find the sum.

5. $\frac{1}{10} + \frac{2}{10} =$ _____

6. $\frac{4}{10} + \frac{3}{10} =$ _____

7. $\frac{3}{5} + \frac{1}{5} =$ _____

8. $\frac{1}{4} + \frac{3}{4} =$ _____

9. $\frac{2}{5} + \frac{1}{5} =$ _____

10. $\frac{7}{12} + \frac{2}{12} =$ _____

11. $\frac{1}{3} + \frac{1}{3} =$ _____

12. $\frac{3}{8} + \frac{3}{8} =$ _____

13. $\frac{1}{4} + \frac{1}{4} =$ _____

14. $\frac{4}{6} + \frac{1}{6} =$ _____

15. $\frac{3}{8} + \frac{4}{8} =$ _____

16. $\frac{6}{12} + \frac{4}{12} =$ _____

## Mixed Review

Add.

17. $3 + 4 + 5 =$ _____

18. $1 + 1 + 9 =$ _____

19. $5 + 8 + 7 =$ _____

Which is greater?

20. 5 feet or 5 inches

21. 2 feet or 2 yards

22. 6 cups or 6 pints

_____

_____

_____

Compare. Write <, >, or = in each ○.

23. $\frac{3}{5} \bigcirc \frac{1}{4}$

24. $\frac{2}{3} \bigcirc \frac{4}{6}$

25. $\frac{1}{8} \bigcirc \frac{3}{9}$

26. $\frac{5}{7} \bigcirc \frac{6}{7}$

27. $\frac{1}{2} \bigcirc \frac{1}{8}$

28. $\frac{2}{5} \bigcirc \frac{3}{4}$

© Harcourt

# Add Fractions

Find the sum. Write the answer in simplest form.

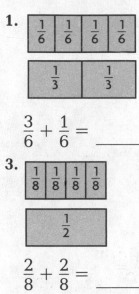

1. $\frac{3}{6} + \frac{1}{6} =$ _____

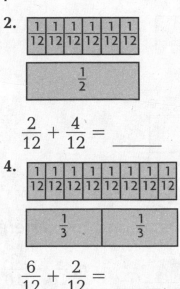

2. $\frac{2}{12} + \frac{4}{12} =$ _____

3. $\frac{2}{8} + \frac{2}{8} =$ _____

4. $\frac{6}{12} + \frac{2}{12} =$ _____

Find the sum. Write the answer in simplest form.
Use fraction bars if you wish.

5. $\frac{1}{6} + \frac{3}{6} =$ _____

6. $\frac{4}{12} + \frac{3}{12} =$ _____

7. $\frac{3}{8} + \frac{3}{8} =$ _____

8. $\frac{1}{4} + \frac{1}{4} =$ _____

9. $\frac{4}{12} + \frac{4}{12} =$ _____

10. $\frac{1}{2} + \frac{1}{2} =$ _____

11. $\frac{1}{6} + \frac{1}{6} =$ _____

12. $\frac{1}{8} + \frac{1}{8} =$ _____

13. $\frac{1}{12} + \frac{1}{12} =$ _____

14. $\frac{1}{10} + \frac{1}{10} =$ _____

15. $\frac{1}{5} + \frac{1}{5} =$ _____

16. $\frac{3}{4} + \frac{1}{4} =$ _____

## Mixed Review

Write a fraction to describe the shaded part.

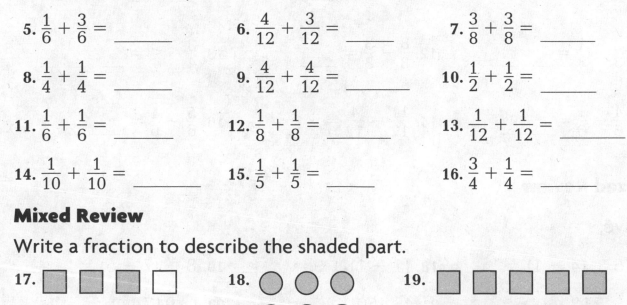

17. _____  18. _____  19. _____

Write the quotient.

20. $30 \div 3 =$ _____  21. $64 \div 8 =$ _____  22. $28 \div 7 =$ _____

# Subtract Fractions

Find the difference.

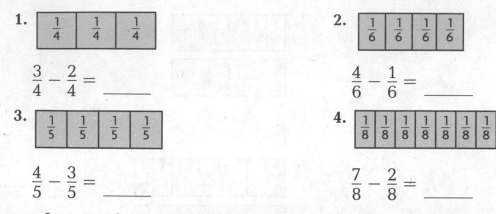

1. $\dfrac{3}{4} - \dfrac{2}{4} =$ _____

2. $\dfrac{4}{6} - \dfrac{1}{6} =$ _____

3. $\dfrac{4}{5} - \dfrac{3}{5} =$ _____

4. $\dfrac{7}{8} - \dfrac{2}{8} =$ _____

Use fraction bars to find the difference.

5. $\dfrac{6}{10} - \dfrac{1}{10} =$ _____

6. $\dfrac{4}{10} - \dfrac{3}{10} =$ _____

7. $\dfrac{3}{5} - \dfrac{1}{5} =$ _____

8. $\dfrac{5}{8} - \dfrac{3}{8} =$ _____

9. $\dfrac{4}{5} - \dfrac{2}{5} =$ _____

10. $\dfrac{7}{12} - \dfrac{2}{12} =$ _____

11. $\dfrac{2}{3} - \dfrac{1}{3} =$ _____

12. $\dfrac{8}{8} - \dfrac{3}{8} =$ _____

13. $\dfrac{3}{4} - \dfrac{2}{4} =$ _____

14. $\dfrac{4}{6} - \dfrac{1}{6} =$ _____

15. $\dfrac{11}{12} - \dfrac{4}{12} =$ _____

16. $\dfrac{5}{6} - \dfrac{4}{6} =$ _____

## Mixed Review

Solve.

17. $5 + (4 - 1) =$ _____

18. $(1 - 1) + 9 =$ _____

19. $8 - (7 - 5) =$ _____

20. $\begin{array}{r} 712 \\ -\ 558 \\ \hline \end{array}$

21. $\begin{array}{r} 450 \\ +\ 388 \\ \hline \end{array}$

22. $\begin{array}{r} 917 \\ -\ 652 \\ \hline \end{array}$

Write the place value of the 2 in each number.

23. 23,957

24. 43,289

25. 808,072

_____

_____

_____

## Subtract Fractions

Compare. Use fraction bars to find the difference. Write the answer in simplest form.

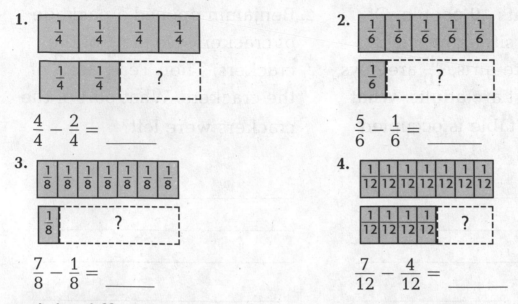

1.

$$\frac{4}{4} - \frac{2}{4} = \underline{\hspace{1cm}}$$

2.

$$\frac{5}{6} - \frac{1}{6} = \underline{\hspace{1cm}}$$

3.

$$\frac{7}{8} - \frac{1}{8} = \underline{\hspace{1cm}}$$

4.

$$\frac{7}{12} - \frac{4}{12} = \underline{\hspace{1cm}}$$

Find the difference. Write the answer in simplest form. Use fraction bars.

5. $\frac{6}{8} - \frac{2}{8} = \underline{\hspace{1cm}}$   6. $\frac{4}{10} - \frac{2}{10} = \underline{\hspace{1cm}}$   7. $\frac{4}{5} - \frac{1}{5} = \underline{\hspace{1cm}}$

8. $\frac{5}{8} - \frac{3}{8} = \underline{\hspace{1cm}}$   9. $\frac{4}{6} - \frac{2}{6} = \underline{\hspace{1cm}}$   10. $\frac{7}{12} - \frac{2}{12} = \underline{\hspace{1cm}}$

11. $\frac{5}{6} - \frac{1}{6} = \underline{\hspace{1cm}}$   12. $\frac{8}{8} - \frac{2}{8} = \underline{\hspace{1cm}}$   13. $\frac{6}{10} - \frac{2}{10} = \underline{\hspace{1cm}}$

14. $\frac{9}{10} - \frac{1}{10} = \underline{\hspace{1cm}}$   15. $\frac{11}{12} - \frac{2}{12} = \underline{\hspace{1cm}}$   16. $\frac{3}{4} - \frac{1}{4} = \underline{\hspace{1cm}}$

## Mixed Review

Add.

17. $\frac{1}{4} + \frac{1}{4} = \underline{\hspace{1cm}}$   18. $\frac{1}{5} + \frac{3}{5} = \underline{\hspace{1cm}}$   19. $\frac{1}{6} + \frac{4}{6} = \underline{\hspace{1cm}}$

Complete.

20. $4 \times \underline{\hspace{1cm}} \times 3 = 12$   21. $5 \times \underline{\hspace{1cm}} \times 8 = 0$   22. $\underline{\hspace{1cm}} \times 8 \times 6 = 48$

# Problem Solving Skill

## Reasonable Answers

Solve. Tell how you know your answer is reasonable.

1. A table seats 10 people. Of the people sitting at the table, $\frac{4}{10}$ are girls, $\frac{4}{10}$ are boys, and the rest are adults. What part of the table is occupied by adults?

_____

_____

_____

_____

_____

2. Benjamin opened a package of crackers. He ate $\frac{3}{8}$ of the crackers. Then Terry ate $\frac{2}{8}$ of the crackers. What part of the crackers were left?

_____

_____

_____

_____

_____

3. Janet colored $\frac{7}{12}$ of her picture red and $\frac{3}{12}$ of her picture green. The rest of the picture was left uncolored. What part of her picture was left uncolored?

_____

_____

_____

4. Michael opened a package of wrapping paper. He used $\frac{1}{4}$ of the paper to wrap a present and $\frac{1}{4}$ of the paper to decorate a box. How much of the paper was left?

_____

_____

_____

## Mixed Review

Solve.

5. $19 - 15 =$ _____

6. $72 \div 9 =$ _____

7. $39 - 27 =$ _____

# Relate Fractions and Decimals

Write the fraction and decimal for the shaded part.

1.

2.

3.

4.

_____ _____ _____ _____

5.

6.

7.

8.

_____ _____ _____ _____

## Mixed Review

Find the quotient.

9. $12 \div 2 =$ _____

10. $16 \div 8 =$ _____

11. $9 \div 3 =$ _____

12. $63 \div 9 =$ _____

13. $50 \div 10 =$ _____

14. $56 \div 7 =$ _____

15. $35 \div 5 =$ _____

16. $24 \div 4 =$ _____

17. $36 \div 4 =$ _____

Solve.

18. $\begin{array}{r} 484 \\ -232 \\ \hline \end{array}$

19. $\begin{array}{r} 795 \\ +496 \\ \hline \end{array}$

20. $\begin{array}{r} 734 \\ -207 \\ \hline \end{array}$

21. $\begin{array}{r} 225 \\ +118 \\ \hline \end{array}$

22. $\begin{array}{r} 8,128 \\ -2,716 \\ \hline \end{array}$

23. $\begin{array}{r} 4,030 \\ +1,812 \\ \hline \end{array}$

24. $\begin{array}{r} 9,235 \\ -2,122 \\ \hline \end{array}$

25. $\begin{array}{r} 5,687 \\ +3,401 \\ \hline \end{array}$

© Harcourt

# Tenths

Use the decimal models to show each amount. Then write
the decimal.

**1.**

**2.**

**3.**

**4.**

$\frac{2}{10}$ _____

$\frac{9}{10}$ _____

$\frac{3}{10}$ _____

$\frac{1}{10}$ _____

Write each fraction or mixed number as a decimal.

**5.** $\frac{4}{10}$ ____   **6.** $\frac{2}{10}$ ____   **7.** $\frac{1}{10}$ ____   **8.** $\frac{9}{10}$ ____   **9.** $1\frac{7}{10}$ ____

Write each decimal as a fraction or mixed number.

**10.** 0.5 ____   **11.** 0.3 ____   **12.** 1.8 ____   **13.** 0.6 ____   **14.** 0.9 ____

## Mixed Review

Compare. Write <, >, or = for each ○.

**15.** $4 \times 7$ ◯ $5 \times 5$

**16.** $3 \times 6$ ◯ $9 \times 2$

**17.** $33$ ◯ $4 \times 8$

**18.** $7 \times 1$ ◯ $14 \times 0$

**19.** $11 \times 4$ ◯ $47$

**20.** $10 \times 2$ ◯ $5 \times 4$

Write each number in expanded form.

**21.** 32,594 _____

**22.** 6,720 _____

**23.** 40,897 _____

**24.** 75,912 _____

# Hundredths

Use the decimal models to show each amount. Then write the decimal.

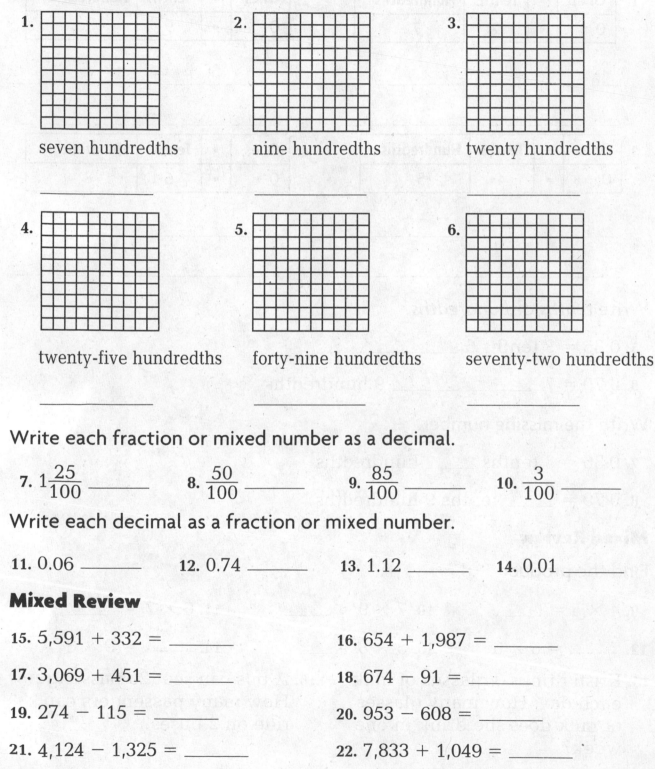

**1.**

seven hundredths

_____

**2.**

nine hundredths

_____

**3.**

twenty hundredths

_____

**4.**

twenty-five hundredths

_____

**5.**

forty-nine hundredths

_____

**6.**

seventy-two hundredths

_____

Write each fraction or mixed number as a decimal.

**7.** $1\frac{25}{100}$ _____   **8.** $\frac{50}{100}$ _____   **9.** $\frac{85}{100}$ _____   **10.** $\frac{3}{100}$ _____

Write each decimal as a fraction or mixed number.

**11.** 0.06 _____   **12.** 0.74 _____   **13.** 1.12 _____   **14.** 0.01 _____

## Mixed Review

**15.** 5,591 + 332 = _____   **16.** 654 + 1,987 = _____

**17.** 3,069 + 451 = _____   **18.** 674 − 91 = _____

**19.** 274 − 115 = _____   **20.** 953 − 608 = _____

**21.** 4,124 − 1,325 = _____   **22.** 7,833 + 1,049 = _____

# Read and Write Decimals

Write the word form and expanded form for each decimal.

1.
| Ones | • | Tenths | Hundredths |
|------|---|--------|------------|
| 0 | • | 2 | 7 |

_____

_____

2.
| Ones | • | Tenths | Hundredths |
|------|---|--------|------------|
| 0 | • | 9 | 1 |

_____

_____

3.
| Ones | • | Tenths | Hundredths |
|------|---|--------|------------|
| 0 | • | 4 | 5 |

_____

_____

4.
| Ones | • | Tenths | Hundredths |
|------|---|--------|------------|
| 0 | • | 6 | 8 |

_____

_____

Write *tenths* or *hundredths*.

5. 0.36 = 3 tenths 6 _____

6. 0.79 = 7 _____ 9 hundredths

Write the missing number.

7. 0.36 = 3 tenths _____ hundredths

8. 0.79 = _____ tenths 9 hundredths

## Mixed Review

Find the product.

9. $4 \times 5 =$ _____

10. $7 \times 9 =$ _____

11. $6 \times 7 =$ _____

12. _____ $= 6 \times 6$

13. $5 \times 8 =$ _____

14. _____ $= 9 \times 3$

15. Kristi drinks 3 glasses of milk each day. How many glasses of milk does she drink in one week?

16. A bus can seat 25 passengers. How many passengers can ride on 2 buses?

_____

_____

Name _____

# Compare and Order Decimals

Compare. Write < or > for each ◯.

1.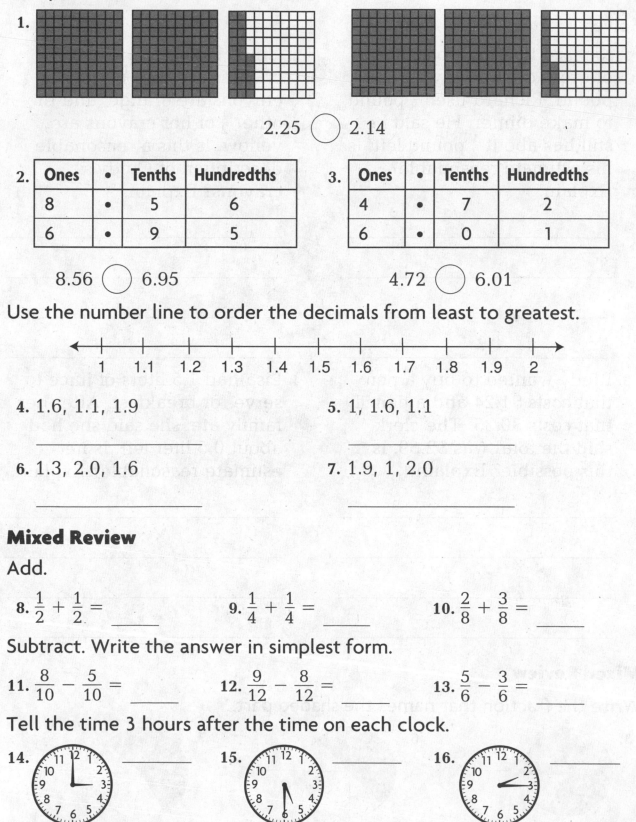

2.25 ◯ 2.14

2.

| Ones | • | Tenths | Hundredths |
|------|---|--------|------------|
| 8 | • | 5 | 6 |
| 6 | • | 9 | 5 |

8.56 ◯ 6.95

3.

| Ones | • | Tenths | Hundredths |
|------|---|--------|------------|
| 4 | • | 7 | 2 |
| 6 | • | 0 | 1 |

4.72 ◯ 6.01

Use the number line to order the decimals from least to greatest.

```
◄——+——+——+——+——+——+——+——+——+——+——+——►
    1   1.1  1.2  1.3  1.4  1.5  1.6  1.7  1.8  1.9   2
```

4. 1.6, 1.1, 1.9

_____

5. 1, 1.6, 1.1

_____

6. 1.3, 2.0, 1.6

_____

7. 1.9, 1, 2.0

_____

## Mixed Review

Add.

8. $\frac{1}{2} + \frac{1}{2} =$ _____

9. $\frac{1}{4} + \frac{1}{4} =$ _____

10. $\frac{2}{8} + \frac{3}{8} =$ _____

Subtract. Write the answer in simplest form.

11. $\frac{8}{10} - \frac{5}{10} =$ _____

12. $\frac{9}{12} - \frac{8}{12} =$ _____

13. $\frac{5}{6} - \frac{3}{6} =$ _____

Tell the time 3 hours after the time on each clock.

14. _____

15. _____

16. _____

© Harcourt

# Problem Solving Skill

## Reasonable Answers

Solve.

**1.** Richard bought a package of ground meat. It weighed a pound. Richard used $\frac{2}{3}$ pound to make dinner. He said he still has about $\frac{1}{2}$ pound left. Is his estimate reasonable? Explain.

_____

_____

_____

_____

**2.** Cindy said that $\frac{1}{2}$ of her crayons are red, $\frac{1}{2}$ of her crayons are orange, and the other $\frac{1}{2}$ of her crayons are yellow. Is this a reasonable description of Cindy's crayons? Explain.

_____

_____

_____

_____

**3.** Brady wanted to buy a pen that costs $1.24 and a pencil that costs $0.35. The clerk said the total was $2.59. Is this possible? Explain.

_____

_____

_____

_____

**4.** Lisa had 1.5 liters of juice to serve for breakfast. After her family ate, she said she had about 0.5 liter left. Is her estimate reasonable? Explain.

_____

_____

_____

_____

## Mixed Review

Write the fraction that names the shaded part.

**5.** 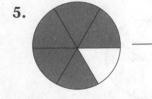 _____

**6.** 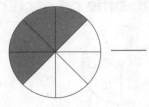 _____

**7.** 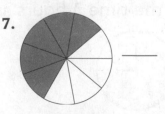 _____

Name _____

# Relate Fractions and Money

Write the amount of money shown. Then write the amount as a fraction of a dollar.

1.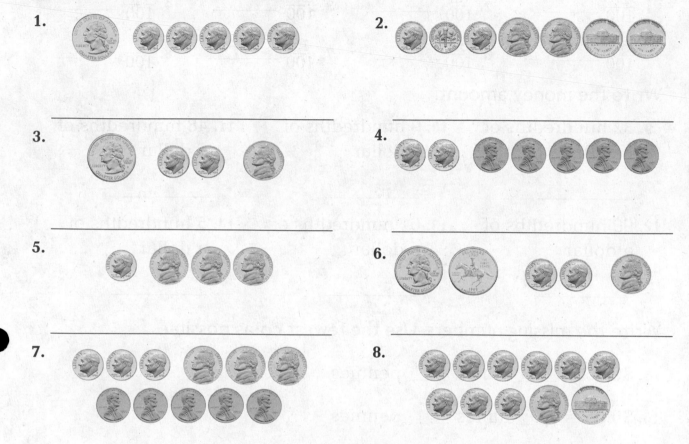

2.

3.

4.

5.

6.

7.

8.

## Mixed Review

Write a decimal to show what part of each decimal square is shaded.

9.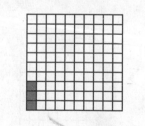

10.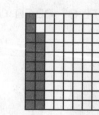

11.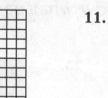

_____ _____ _____

Find the quotient.

12. $54 \div 9 =$ _____  13. $50 \div 5 =$ _____  14. $20 \div 5 =$ _____

© Harcourt

# Relate Decimals and Money

Write the money amount for each fraction of a dollar.

1. $\frac{20}{100}$ _____     2. $\frac{62}{100}$ _____     3. $\frac{25}{100}$ _____     4. $\frac{78}{100}$ _____

5. $\frac{55}{100}$ _____     6. $\frac{50}{100}$ _____     7. $\frac{15}{100}$ _____     8. $\frac{9}{100}$ _____

Write the money amount.

9. 32 hundredths of a dollar

10. 9 hundredths of a dollar

11. 48 hundredths of a dollar

_____     _____     _____

12. 99 hundredths of a dollar

13. 61 hundredths of a dollar

14. 5 hundredths of a dollar

_____     _____     _____

Write the missing numbers. Use the fewest coins possible.

15. $0.36 = ____ dimes ____ pennies

16. $0.05 = ____ dimes ____ pennies

17. $0.64 = ____ dimes ____ pennies

18. $0.14 = ____ dimes ____ pennies

## Mixed Review

Write a fraction to show what part of each decimal model is shaded.

19. 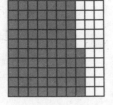     20. 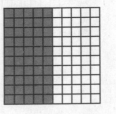     21.

_____     _____     _____